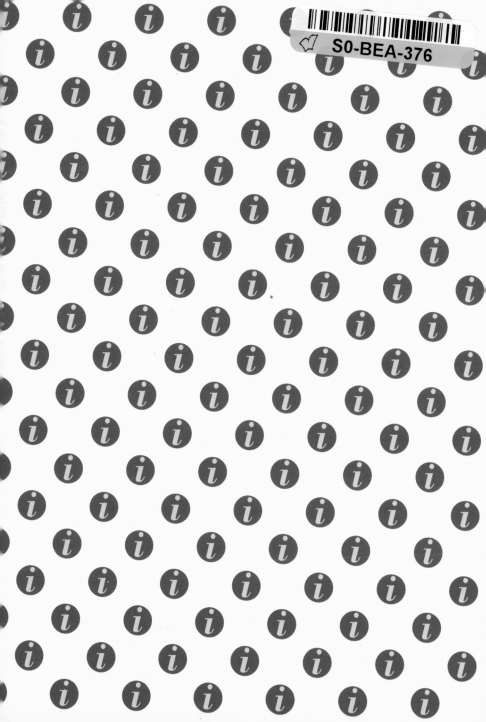

SO-BEA-376

Shells

The illustrated Identifier to over 140 species

Shells

The illustrated Identifier to over 140 species

Fred Woodward

CHARTWELL
BOOKS, INC.

A QUINTET BOOK

Published by
CHARTWELL BOOKS, INC.
A division of **BOOK SALES INC.**
114 Northfield Avenue
Edison, New Jersey 08837

ISBN 1–55521–841–5

Reprinted 1998

This book was designed and produced by
Quintet Publishing Limited
6 Blundell Street
London N7 9BH

Creative Director: Richard Dewing
Designer: Stuart Walden
Project Editor: Damian Thompson
Editor: Lydia Darbyshire
Photographer: Paul Forrester

Special thanks to Ken Wye of the
Eaton Shell Shop, London

Typeset in Great Britain by
Central Southern Typesetters, Eastbourne
Manufactured in Singapore by
Bright Arts Pte Limited
Printed in Hong Kong by Sing Cheong Printing Co. Ltd.

CONTENTS

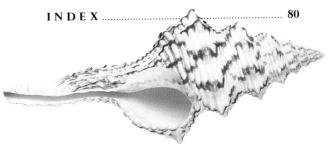

INTRODUCTION

M an has used both shells, and the animals that produce them for over 6,000 years, and their remains have been found in archaeological sites dating from at least 4000BC. The remains of shells such as limpets, oysters and land snails have been found in Bronze Age settlements, and the Romans are known to have farmed oysters for food. Bronze Age sites in Africa have yielded bivalve shells that were clearly used as scrapers. Museums throughout the world contain evidence of the early use of shells in the production of items as diverse as drinking utensils to fish-hooks, but traces of shells such as cowries and conches and fragments of mother-of-pearl suggest that shells were also esteemed for their decorative qualities.

The rock shells, the purple dye murex (*Bolinus brandaris*) and the trunk murex (*Hexaplex trunculus*) were used by the ancient Romans to make Tyrian purple dye, which was used to colour imperial and ecclesiastical robes. Cuttle-fish (*Sepia* spp.), which are molluscs, were used from earliest times as a source of ink – the creatures eject a black fluid when they are pursued.

Cowries, especially the species *Cypraea annulus* and *C. moneta,* were used in many parts of Asia, central Africa, Malaysia and the islands of the Indian Ocean as a type of currency. The first Chinese metallic coins, which date from about 600BC, are in the form of small cowries. North American Indians used beads – known as wampum – made from bivalve shells and strung together as money, decoration or as mnemonic patterns. Chieftains in Polynesia used the

BELOW LEFT A characteristic Victorian decorative ornament, c1880, made by wiring shells together to form flowers.

BELOW The Lesser or Curled Octopus, Eledone cirrosa (Lamarck), a member of the Cephalopoda, whose ink-sac, like that of the squids, was used as a source of "Sepia Ink".

highly prized golden cowrie (*Cypraea aurantium*) as a badge of rank. The helmet shells, especially the bullmouth helmet (*Cypraecassis rufa*), were used for the manufacture of cameos in the jewellery trade, craftsmen carving through the layers to create images and patterns.

The Indian chank shell (*Turbinella pyrum*) is sacred to the Hindu god Vishnu and is used in ceremonial and religious rites. Extremely rare left-hand or sinistral forms are much sought after and command high prices among devout Hindus. The aptly named trumpet triton (*Charonia tritonis*), the largest species in the triton family, is often used, once the apex has been removed, as a trumpet to call the faithful to prayer.

In the West, the scallop was the emblem of St James of Compostela, because, said Erasmus, the shores of the adjacent sea abounds in them. In time, the shell was adopted as an emblem by pilgrims to the shrine and then by pilgrims in general. Pilgrims to Santiago de Compostela used to wear a scallop, or cockle, shell in their hats. The polished side of the shell was scratched, often with some crude drawing associated with the pilgrimage. Blessed by the priest, the shells were considered as amulets against spiritual foes.

BELOW LEFT A seventeenth-century, carved, Pearly Nautilus shell mounted in silver-gilt and coral, probably made in Holland or Germany.

BELOW The shell of a large Helmet shell with its outer surface carved to form a cameo. The large size of this example indicates it was probably intended as an advert for either a dealer or producer of cameos.

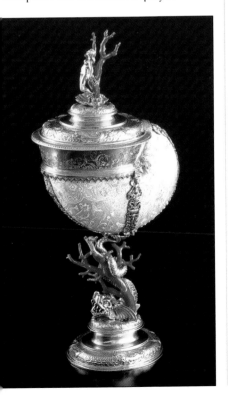

MOLLUSCAN BIOLOGY

Molluscs are found in a wide variety of habitats, from the deepest ocean basins to the highest mountain tops, and there is great diversity of form not only among classes but also among species of the same family.

GASTROPODA

This class contains over three-quarters of living molluscs. Gastropods have a soft body and large foot, which are normally enclosed in a hard, protective shell. Although gastropod shells are often spirally coiled, some species have dome-, cap- or cone-shaped shells. The spiral shells are usually coiled into a helix, but some are formed into a flat plane, while others open out into an irregular, twisted shape. Most gastropods are active and highly mobile, and they are found in the sea, in freshwater and on land. There are approximately 30,000 described species, including limpets, top shells, cowries, cones and volutes.

In some species of gastropod the shell is reduced, internal or absent; in others various organs are reduced or absent – the operculum, for example, is not always present.

Many gastropods possess a radula, a rasping tongue that is used in feeding from vegetable or animal matter. In some specialized species, the radula is used to bore a hole in the shell of prey. The radular teeth of cone shells, members of the Conidae family, are modified to form hollow harpoon-like barbs through which a poison is shot into the prey. The species with the largest apertures are thought to be most dangerous, and several human deaths are reported to have been caused by careless handling of live specimens.

Respiration is normally by means of gill-like filaments, although in terrestrial forms these are modified to form a lung-like chamber.

The sexes are usually separate, although in some species the creature may be both sexes, either simultaneously or changing from one sex to the other through age or in response to environmental factors. Development may be from eggs, from which free-swimming, intermediate-stage larvae, known as veligers, emerge or direct.

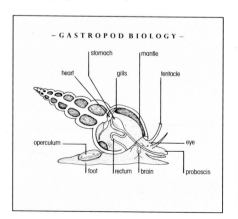

– GASTROPOD BIOLOGY –

stomach, mantle, heart, gills, tentacle, operculum, eye, foot, rectum, brain, proboscis

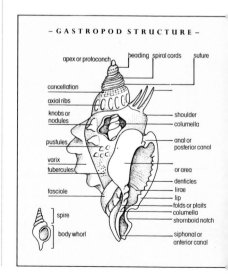

– GASTROPOD STRUCTURE –

apex or protoconch, beading, spiral cords, suture, cancellation, axial ribs, knobs or nodules, pustules, varix, tubercules, fasciole, spire, body whorl, shoulder, columella, anal or posterior canal, or area, denticles, lirae, lip, folds or plaits, columella, stromboid notch, siphonal or anterior canal

BIVALVIA

The shells of bivalves are composed of two valves which vary considerably, but in all species they are joined along their dorsal surface by an elastic ligament, which causes the valves to open. To counteract this, the valves are held together by strong muscles that are attached to the inner shell surface and that produce the characteristic scars. The hinge structure may or may not have interlocking, tooth-like projections.

The animal lacks a true head and radula and feeds by trapping organic particles as they pass over its gills. The tongue-like foot, which protrudes from the front end, is often comparatively large and is used for loco-motion, although species such as oysters become permanently attached to the sub-strate by means of silky threads produced by a byssal gland in the foot. Inhalant and exhalant siphons, in varying degrees of complexity, are situated at the posterior end.

In most species the sexes are separate, but some species are hermaphrodite, and

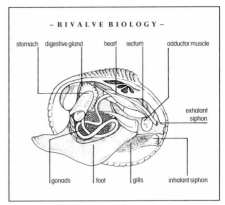

– BIVALVE BIOLOGY –

stomach digestive gland heart rectum adductor muscle

exhalant siphon

gonads foot gills inhalant siphon

some change sex over time. Eggs and sperm may be liberated into the surrounding water via the exhalant siphons, and the fertilized eggs develop into free-swimming veligers, which develop into bivalves. In some species, eggs are brooded within the shell cavity.

BELOW A live example of the Painted Top,
Calliostoma zizyphinum, *which is widely distributed in shallow rocky areas throughout western Europe.*

– CLASSIFICATION AND NOMENCLATURE –

Living things are divided into two major groups – plants and animals. These groups are themselves subdivided. Animals are divided into two groups: vertebrates – ie, creatures that have a backbone, such as fish, birds and mammals – and invertebrates – ie, creatures that do not have a backbone, such as jellyfish, insects and corals. These major categories are further divided into groups known as phyla, these divisions being based on the presence or absence of common features – jointed legs, for example.

Molluscs, which do not have backbones, are invertebrates, and they form a phylum – Mollusca – the members of which have unsegmented bodies and, normally, shells. This large phylum, which is second in numerical size only to the Arthropoda (insects), is subdivided into smaller groups or classes. These classes are further divided according to combinations of shell and animal characteristics into subclass, order, super family, family, subfamily, genus and, finally, species. The species name is unique to a particular animal. It is based on the binomial system devised by the Swedish naturalist Carl Linnaeus (1707–78). Each species has two latinized names. The first – generic – name denotes the group or genus to

which this animal and its close relatives belong.

The second – specific – name denotes the particular group within the genus. The species name is followed by the name of the person who first described the shell together with the date of publication. For example, the common European or edible cockle is classified as follows:

Phylum	Mollusca
Class	Bivalvia
Subclass	Heterodonta
Order	Veneroida
Super family	Cardioidea
Family	Cardiidae
Subfamily	Laevicardiinae
Genus	*Cerastoderma*
Species	*edule*
Author	Linnaeus
Date published	1758

This information is not only unique to the animal concerned but is also internationally recognized. Popular names tend to vary from place to place – there may even be local variations within a country – but specific names are universal, and their use will prevent any misunderstandings about which precise shells are meant.

CEPHALOPODA

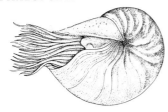

This group contains creatures with a well-developed head with eyes. They have eight or ten sucker-bearing arms or tentacles and a horny, beak-like structure, which is used for tearing their prey. All are carnivorous. The class includes octopuses and squids, but only the Nautilidae and Argonautidae are of interest to shell collectors. The head and foot are united, and there are gills and sensory organs. In most species the sexes are separate and there is no free-swimming larval or veliger stage. Instead, the fully developed embryo emerges from the egg.

Nautilids have external shells. Argonauts, on the other hand, are octopus-like creatures that do not have true shells. The "shell", which is produced by the female of the species, is only loosely attached to the body and its main function is to hold the eggs.

SCAPHOPODA

The members of this class are commonly known as tusk shells, and they are found throughout the world in temperate to tropical seas. There are over 1,000 species. They have hollow, tubular, tusk-shaped shells, which are open at both ends. Some species have a notch or slit in the posterior portion of the shell or a small terminal "pipe". The shell tapers along its length, and the creature's foot emerges from the larger, lower opening.

Scaphopods live buried in sand inside their tubular shells. The animal feeds by sucking in water bearing organic particles through the smaller open end of the shell, which protrudes above the sand's surface. There is no distinct head, eyes or gills, but the foot is large and there is a well-developed radula. They feed mainly on protozoa and other microscopic organisms. The sexes are separate, and the larval form has a pair of valve-like structures that fuse together to produce the adult shell. These are usually deep-water species, and living specimens are seldom seen. However, the empty shells are regularly washed up on beaches.

POLYPLACOPHORA

This class, also known as Amphineura, contains the chitons or coat-of-mail shells, whose strange, segmented shells of eight plates are held together by a leathery band or girdle and which resemble woodlice when they curl up for protection. There are believed to be between 600 and 1,000 species, all of which are vegetarians.

These species live in the intertidal zone and in offshore waters, generally in rock crevices or beneath rocks. They possess a well-developed radula, a large foot but no tentacles or eyes. The sexes are separate. A few species have free-swimming veliger, but in most species the mother protects her young until they are capable of fending for themselves.

– HOW TO USE THIS BOOK –

The shells in this book are divided up within their 5 major classes – Gastropoda, Bivalvia, Polyplacophora, Cephalopoda and Scaphopoda – of which the gastropods and bivalves take up the majority of the book. The order of classification is Class, Super Family, Family, and Species. Each class is subdivided into Super Families which are further subdivided into Families. Within their families individual species of shells are described and illustrated. Each Super Family is colour coded, and any Families or Species within it are coded in a lighter shade of that colour.

1 Superfamily classification – Stromboidea (darker shading).

SUPER FAMILY
STROMBOIDEA

2 Family – Common name – Pelican's Foot shells Classification name – Aporrhaidae (lighter shading).

PELICAN'S FOOT SHELLS
family Aporrhaidae

Pelican's foot shells occur in sandy mud in the deeper, cooler waters of the north Atlantic and Mediterranean. There are six living species, but many fossil forms are known. The name derives from the appearance of the flattened lip of the aperture of mature specimens. The operculum is small in all the species, but the number and shape of the extensions may vary widely, even within species.

3 General description of the particular family of shells.

4

5

2in
5cm

6

4 Habitat depth. Figures are approximate and some species are found at more than one depth.

A ☐ extends to about 83ft (25m)

B ◩ between 83ft and 495ft (25–150m)

C ◪ between 495ft and 1,650ft (150–500m)

5 Average size of mature shell.

6 Rarity.

D � Abundant. Readily available in both accessible collecting areas and commercial sources.

E ✖ Common. Not always available commercially. Shell's habitat perhaps specilized or not easily accessible.

F ◼ Rare. Seldom available commercially and therefore expensive and sought after. Could be deep or dangerous-water species or those living in inaccessible habitats.

7 The scientific (specific) name of the individual species within the family – *Aporrhais pespelicani* (lighter shading).

8 The name of the author and the date of publication – (Linnaeus 1758). The author's name and date sometimes appear in parentheses. This is because the shell has, since its first publication, been recognized, accepted and reclassified into another genus.

9 The common name – that is, the name by which a shell is widely known – Common pelican's foot. However, to avoid confusion it is always wise to include the specific name as common names can vary widely from place to place, and it is not unknown for the same common name to be applied to two quite distinct species.

10 A brief general description of the shell, including diagnostic information that will enable identification to be made.

11 The shell's distribution – that is, the area or areas in the world where the shell is likely to be found.

APORRHAIS PESPELICANI

AUTHORITY: (Linnaeus 1758)
COMMON NAME: Common pelican's foot
GENERAL DESCRIPTION: The aperture of the common pelican's foot is extended to produce four finger-like outgrowths, resembling a bird's foot, hence its common name. The whorls are angular and nodulose. The shells are usually cream coloured or off-white, although some may be darker brown. The species is widely distributed, being found from the Mediterranean to Norway, inhabiting deeper muddy offshore areas down to depths in excess of 450ft (140m).
DISTRIBUTION: Mediterranean; northwest Europe

MARINE REGIONS OF THE WORLD

HABITAT AND DISTRIBUTION

Marine molluscs occur throughout the world and in almost any environment where the water offers an adequate supply of food. Most species, including the most highly coloured and patterned, live in shallow waters, many thriving in sand or muddy habitats, or burrowing into sandy substrates.

The habitat in which a shell is discovered is often an important clue to its identity. In this book shell habitats are described as **inter-** **tidal,** which refers to the area between the extreme high-tide and extreme low-water marks, or as **subtidal,** which is in the shallow water from below the extreme low-water mark down to the edge of the continental slope. Deep-water species are known as **abyssal.**

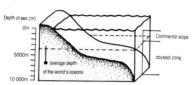

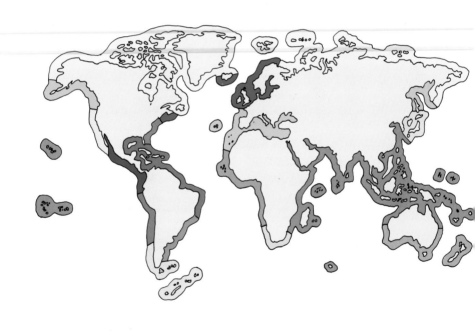

ARCTIC

ALEUTIAN

AUSTRALIAN

BOREAL

CALIFORNIAN

CARIBBEAN

INDO-PACIFIC

JAPONIC

MAGELLANIC

MEDITERRANEAN

PANAMIC

PATAGONIAN

PERUVIAN

SOUTH AFRICAN

TRANSATLANTIC

WEST AFRICAN

– CLEANING AND STORAGE –

Shells purchased from dealers or obtained through exchange will normally be ready to be placed directly into your collection. Specimens that you have collected yourself may require further treatment.

The soft body parts of live-collected material must be preserved or removed before they begin to decompose and putrefy. If you wish to preserve the animal, it should be drowned by being placed in freshly boiled water, which will cause it to relax and come out of its shell, and then placed in a preservative. Suitable preservatives are a 10 per cent solution of formalin mixed with a few drops of glycerine, industrial methylated spirits or 70 per cent alcohol, although this last is difficult to obtain unless you have access to a laboratory. Animals can be removed by being boiled for a short time.

Bivalves are easily removed from their shells, but you will need a pin to deal with gastropods. Take care to remove and preserve the operculum if one is present. This should be kept separately or stuck to a piece of cotton wool and inserted into the shell aperture.

Encrustations on the shell can be removed with a wire brush or in a weak solution of acetic acid (white wine vinegar). Some collectors prefer to retain such "blemishes", since they provide additional information about the animal's habitat.

Storage will depend on your personal taste and also on any limitations imposed by space and finances. Cupboards or cabinets with shallow drawers are preferable, and individual shells can be kept in plastic- or glass-topped boxes, tubes or cardboard trays. Each shell should be numbered and accompanied by a label bearing all the relevant information, including the scientific and common names, the date and place of collection, the name of the collector, the name of the identifier, preservation methods and any other appropriate information. This information should, ideally, also be kept in a loose-leaf file or notebook.

Plastic tweezers for picking up small shells.

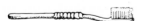

Toothbrush for removing sand or brushing shell sand into plastic bags or containers.

Pencil or indelible pen for writing notes.

Hand lens, preferably magnification × 10, for examining small shells.

Notebook for field notes

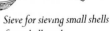

Sieve for sieving small shells from shell sand.

Sharp knife for prising shells off rocks or out of crevices.

CLASS
GASTROPODA

This class contains molluscs that possess a soft body and a large foot, which is normally enclosed within a single, protective coiled shell. There are some 30,000 described species of gastropod, including limpets, cowries, cones and volutes.

SUPER FAMILY
PLEUROTOMARIOIDEA

SLIT SHELLS
family Pleurotomariidae

The ancestors of this ancient molluscan family occur as Cambrian fossils, formed some 600 million years ago, and they too possessed the characteristic slit on the body whorl and a horny operculum. All recent species are vegetarians, and they normally inhabit waters to depths of 2,000ft (600m), for which reason they are rarely seen in amateur collections. The shells are comparatively large and usually round or conical.

PEROTROCHUS WESTRALIS

AUTHORITY: Whitehead 1987
COMMON NAME: West Australian slit shell
GENERAL DESCRIPTION: This recently described species has a large, top-shaped shell with eight or nine whorls, the body whorl has the characteristic slit. The shell is a pale beige colour, decorated with a few faint orange streaks. It is sometimes trawled off west Australia at depths of 1,500ft (450m).

Another recently described and closely related species, *Perotrochus tangaroana* Bouchet and Metivier 1982, has been dredged at a depth of about 2,000ft (600m) from Lau Ridge and the North Cape Rise off New Zealand.
DISTRIBUTION: West Australia.

ABALONES

family Haliotidae

Abalones, which are also known as ormers or sea ears, are vegetarians. There are about 100 species distributed throughout the world from low-tide level to depths of several hundred feet. The shells are flattened and ear shaped, and each one has a series of holes on the body whorl through which water and waste products are passed. The pearly interior, which bears a single, central muscle scar, is often used as a source of mother-of-pearl. The animal lacks an operculum. Abalones are often used as food, and the larger species from California are farmed for this purpose.

SUPER FAMILY

FISSURELLOIDEA

KEYHOLE LIMPETS

family Fissurellidae

The members of the Fissurellidae family are commonly known as keyhole limpets because there is a hole at the apex of the conical shell in the majority of species. They are found throughout the world on rocky shores and among coral. They are fairly primitive molluscs with no operculum. All the members of the family are vegetarians.

ALIOTIS RUBER

THORITY: Leach 1814
MMON NAME: Ruber abalone
NERAL DESCRIPTION: The spire of *Haliotis ruber* is n eroded, exposing the white, highly iridescent pearly er beneath. The upper surface is a pale red colour. It is haps the best known Australian abalone, and it is nmonly found on rocks and in crevices from extreme low-level downwards throughout the shallow waters off south tralia.
STRIBUTION: South Australia; Tasmania

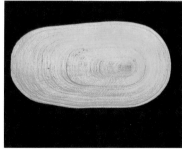

SCUTUS ANTIPODES

AUTHORITY: Montfort 1810
COMMON NAME: Roman shield limpet
GENERAL DESCRIPTION: The Roman shield limpet is atypical of the family because it does not have an apical hole. Its generic and common names derive from the shell's supposed resemblance to a Roman shield, *scutum*. It is common on rocks in the intertidal zone of New Zealand and grows on average to 2in (5cm), although specimens up to 3½in (9cm) have been found. The ribbed exterior, which clearly reveals the shell's growth stages, is yellowish-beige; the interior is white.
DISTRIBUTION: South Australia; north New Zealand

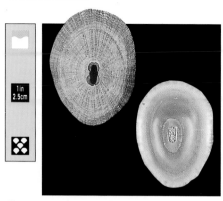

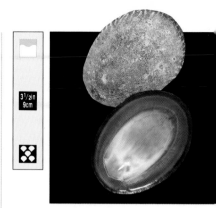

FISSURELLA BARBADENSIS

AUTHORITY: (Gmelin 1791)
COMMON NAME: Barbados keyhole limpet
GENERAL DESCRIPTION: The Barbados keyhole limpet, with its oval shape, pale green interior and characteristic figure-of-eight apical hole, is well known to collectors. The outer shell surface is often coated with lime deposits, which can obscure the delicate radiating ridging. It is common on intertidal rocks from south Florida to Brazil, and is, as its name suggests, especially abundant in the West Indies.
DISTRIBUTION: South Florida to Brazil; West Indies

LOTTIA GIGANTEA

AUTHORITY: (Sowerby 1834)
COMMON NAME: Giant owl limpet
GENERAL DESCRIPTION: The upper surface of this la flattened, oval shell is patterned with irregular blotches and normally heavily encrusted. The interior exhibits an oval, pa blue or white muscle scar, which is surrounded by the uniform deep brown and glossy inner surface, which is, in turn, edged by a black marginal band. The species occurs o rocks just below the high-tide mark.
DISTRIBUTION: California to Mexico

SUPER FAMILY

PATELLOIDEA

TRUE LIMPETS

families Acmaeidae
and Lottiidae

The members of these two families have limpet-like shells with a horseshoe-shaped muscle scar on the porcellaneous interior, which is often brightly coloured. Most species occur intertidally on rocky shores, but they may also be discovered on seaweed or even on other shells. They are found throughout the world but are particularly common on the Pacific coasts of North America.

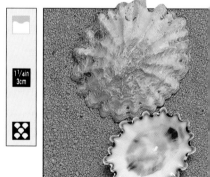

PATELLOIDEA ALTICOSTAT

AUTHORITY: (Angas 1865)
COMMON NAME: High ribbed limpet
GENERAL DESCRIPTION: This widespread species is usually found in association with the green seaweed ulva, o which it feeds. The upper surface has about 20 radial ridges, but these are often hidden beneath encrusting algae. The inside is white or off-white with a pale brown, central muscle scar. Some shells also have a black marginal border.
DISTRIBUTION: South Australia

SUPER FAMILY
TROCHOIDEA

TOP SHELLS

family Trochidae

The hundreds of species in this family have a worldwide distribution. The small to large conical shells are covered by a skin or periostracum and often have radial or spiral sculpture. The inner shell layer is pearly, and the animal has a corneous operculum. Top shells feed on seaweed and occur in large numbers on coral reefs or among seaweed on rocky shores.

CITTARIUM PICA

AUTHORITY: (Linnaeus 1758)
COMMON NAME: Magpie shell
GENERAL DESCRIPTION: This well-known species, with its thick, heavy shell traversed by striking, wavy black and cream bands, has a wide umbilicus. It has a circular, greenish-black, horny operculum. The species is found in subtidal rocky areas throughout the Caribbean, where it is collected as an ingredient for soup.
DISTRIBUTION: Caribbean

ЛISCHKEA IMPERIALIS

UTHORITY: (Dall 1881)
OMMON NAME: Imperial top shell
ENERAL DESCRIPTION: This is an extremely rare pecies. The thin, rather dirty-looking beige outer surface ontrasts with the highly iridescent pearly interior. The five or ix whorls are decorated by four or five rows of spiny nodules. occurs at depths between 200 and 1,000 feet (60–300m) nd is sometimes caught in fish or lobster traps. The shell ustrated was obtained from off Carlisle Bay, Barbados, at a epth of 1,000ft (300m).
ISTRIBUTION: Off Florida and the Caribbean

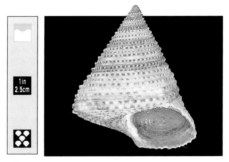

CALLIOSTOMA ANNULATUM

AUTHORITY: (Lightfoot 1786)
COMMON NAME: Ringed top shell
GENERAL DESCRIPTION: This shell has for long been considered a collector's item, and specimens were fetching prices of £3–4 even in the early 1800s. Although it is comparatively common, it is still greatly sought after by modern collectors. The shell's exquisite appearance results from each whorl being sculptured by coloured spiral beading to produce red and white dots, which contrast with a spiral band of lavender immediately above the suture. The background is a yellowish-brown. It occurs offshore at depths varying from 3 to 60 feet (1–20m).
DISTRIBUTION: Alaska to southern California

TURBAN SHELLS
family Turbinidae

Turban shells contain several hundred species, which are divided into three subfamilies, the dolphin shells or Angariinae, the true turbans or Turbininae and the star shells or Astraeinae. In general the shells are medium to large, and are solid and top shaped. They may or may not bear long, curved spines. The interior is pearly, and the columella is smooth. The operculum is normally solid and calcareous. The species are herbivores, and they occur in warm inter- and subtidal waters among seaweed or on rocky or coral reefs.

PHEASANT SHELLS
families Phasionellidae and Tricoliidae

Pheasant shells possess smooth, brightly coloured exteriors, which occur in a wide range of patterns and colours. They differ from trochids and turbans in having a porcellaneous, non-pearly interior. The pear-shaped aperture has a chalky but smooth operculum. Most species are vegetarian, and are widely distributed in temperate and warm waters.

3in
7cm

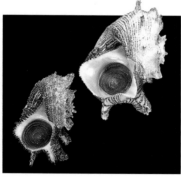

2in
5cm

ANGARIA TYRIA

AUTHORITY: (Reeve 1842)
COMMON NAME: Tyria delphinula
GENERAL DESCRIPTION: The tyria delphinula belongs to the dolphin shells and, like the other members of the subfamily, it has a thin and corneous operculum. The shells are highly variable in form, but they have well-developed spines. This species is found on shallow coral reefs. The larger of the shells illustrated was obtained from off northwest Australia; the smaller one probably comes from the Philippines.
DISTRIBUTION: Southwest Pacific; Australia

PHASIANELLA AUSTRALIS

AUTHORITY: (Gmelin 1791)
COMMON NAME: Australian pheasant
GENERAL DESCRIPTION: The Australian pheasant shell, which is also sometimes known as the painted lady, exhibits considerable variation in colour and pattern, as can readily be seen from the examples illustrated. The early apical whorls are not normally patterned. This, the largest and perhaps most attractive of the pheasant shells, is worthy of a place in any collection. The species may be found among seaweed in shallow waters around south Australia and Tasmania.
DISTRIBUTION: South Australia; Tasmania

SUPER FAMILY

NERITOIDEA

NERITES

family Neritidae

These small to medium, thick and rather short-spired shells have a thickened outer lip, which is often toothed. The umbilicus is absent. They have a calcareous operculum, which has a tooth-like projection on its inner surface. They are herbivorous. Nerites are mostly found in the intertidal zone, with some species occurring in brackish or fresh water. There are about 50 species in all.

SUPER FAMILY

LITTORINOIDEA

PERIWINKLES

family Littorinidae

Periwinkles are small to medium-sized shells that are found throughout the world. There are at least 50 species, although some authorities say there are 100. They have a circular, thin, horny operculum but no umbilicus. All are vegetarians, feeding on seaweed and other algae. The sexes are separate, the females shedding their eggs directly into water or laying gelatinous egg masses.

1/4in
0.7cm

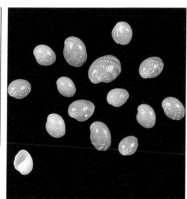

1in
2.5cm

SMARAGDIA VIRIDIS

AUTHORITY: (Linnaeus 1758)
COMMON NAME: Emerald nerite
GENERAL DESCRIPTION: This minute species is reservedly popular among collectors, for its bright green coloration is attractively crossed by numerous fine white axial lines. The spire is low, and the body whorl is greatly enlarged. It lives in shallow water, especially on eel-grass beds.
DISTRIBUTION: Southeast Florida; West Indies; Bermuda

LITTORINA LITTOREA

AUTHORITY: (Linnaeus 1758)
COMMON NAME: Common periwinkle
GENERAL DESCRIPTION: The common periwinkle has a robust, rounded shell, with a rather short spire. It is grey in colour and may exhibit fine spiral striations. The aperture and columella are white and smooth, and the corneous operculum is dark brown. It occurs among seaweed on rocky shores and is in great demand for food.
DISTRIBUTION: West Europe; northeast North America

SUPER FAMILY

CERITHIOIDEA

CERITH SHELLS

family Cerithiidae

All species are vegetarian. The small to medium, elongated shells are often spirally striated or nodular. The aperture is set at an oblique angle and extends as a recurved siphonal canal. The thin, horny operculum is subcircular and has only a few whorls. Ceriths are mainly distributed in the tropics in intertidal and shallow subtidal areas, where they are found on seaweed or among coral debris, feeding on algae and detritus. A few species are found in the cooler waters off Europe.

LITTORINA SCABRA ANGULIFERA

AUTHORITY: (Lamarck 1822)
COMMON NAME: Angulate periwinkle
GENERAL DESCRIPTION: This species appears to have two colour forms. Shells that come from the Caribbean are generally yellowish or white and are mottled with light and dark brown streaks. Australian specimens, such as the examples from Yeppoon, Queensland, illustrated here, tend to be uniform browns, pinks or yellows, and they are lighter in weight with sharp spiral ribs.
DISTRIBUTION: Southeast United States to Brazil; Bermuda; Queensland, Australia

CERITHIUM CUMINGI

AUTHORITY: A. Adams 1855
COMMON NAME: Cumming's cerithium
GENERAL DESCRIPTION: This species has a rather weakly nodulose shell, and the beige background is overlaid by flecks of darker brown. The shells can be locally common on sand or mud in shallow water. The two specimens shown here come from Port Hedland, on the west coast of Australia, and the right-hand example illustrates the typical cerithid aperture and operculum.
DISTRIBUTION: Indo-Pacific islands; north and west Australia

BELL CLAPPERS

family Campanilidae

The bell clapper is the sole survivor of a formerly large family, which included over 700 species, including one species found in the deposits of the Paris Basin, *Campanula giganteum,* which grew to a length of at least 20in (50cm).

HORN SHELLS

family Potamididae

Horn shells, or mud creepers as they are also known, inhabit tropical muddy or brackish water areas, such as mangrove swamps, where they occur in large numbers, feeding on marine detritus and algae. The animal has a thin, horny, many-coiled, circular operculum.

6in 15cm

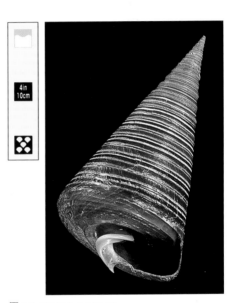

4in 10cm

TELESCOPIUM TELESCOPIUM

AUTHORITY: (Linnaeus 1758)
COMMON NAME: Telescope shell
GENERAL DESCRIPTION: The telescope shell is found in mangrove mud flats throughout the Indo-Pacific area. It is a popular shell with collectors, its tall, straight-sided outline giving it a top-like appearance. The whorls are spirally grooved, and the base of the columella is twisted like a corkscrew. These comparatively heavy shells are usually a uniform dark brown, with a contrasting ridge of light brown, grey or white.
DISTRIBUTION: Indo-Pacific

CAMPANILE SYMBOLICUM

AUTHORITY: Irelade 1917
COMMON NAME: Bell clapper
GENERAL DESCRIPTION: The bell clapper has an operculum, and its chalky-white shell has a fossil-like look. The whorls are devoid of patterning, but they are sculptured by faint spiral grooves. The apex of most specimens tends to be broken off. It is restricted to southwest Australia and a vegetarian.
DISTRIBUTION: Southwest Australia

SCREW SHELLS
family Turritellidae

There are more than 100 species of screw shells distributed throughout the world. They inhabit sandy and muddy offshore waters, where they feed upon marine detritus and algae. The animal has a chitinous operculum and no siphonal canal, and the shells are remarkable for their shape rather than their colour.

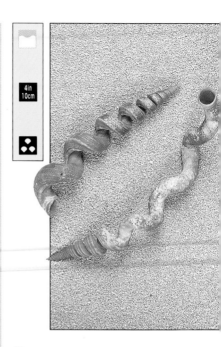

4in
10cm

VERMICULARIA SPIRATA

AUTHORITY: (Philippi 1836)
COMMON NAME: Caribbean worm shell
GENERAL DESCRIPTION: The Caribbean or West Indian worm shell derives its name from the fact that its normal coiled turritellid shell, which is very similar to a screw shell, becomes open and irregular after about six whorls, the resulting shell resembling certain marine worms. It occurs in southeast Florida, the West Indies and Bermuda, where it lives among shallow-water sponges.
DISTRIBUTION: South Florida; West Indies; Bermuda

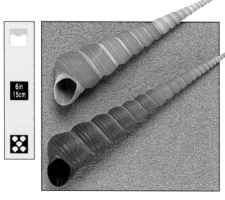

6in
15cm

TURRITELLA TEREBRA

AUTHORITY: (Linnaeus 1758)
COMMON NAME: Common screw shell
GENERAL DESCRIPTION: The common screw shell, or tower screw shell, as it is sometimes known, occurs in the sandy, subtidal muds of the Indo-Pacific area. They may be up to 30 whorls, which are ornamented with a series of fine, rounded spiral ribs. The shell is normally pale to dark brown in colour. The aperture is round, and the horny operculum is thin, circular and multispiral, with a central nucleus.
DISTRIBUTION: Indo-Pacific

SUPER FAMILY
STROMBOIDEA

PELICAN'S FOOT SHELLS
family Aporrhaidae

Pelican's foot shells occur in sandy mud in the deeper, cooler waters of the north Atlantic and Mediterranean. There are six living species, but many fossil forms are known. The name derives from the appearance of the flattened lip of the aperture of mature specimens. The operculum is small in all the species, but the number and shape of the extensions may vary widely, even within species.

CONCH SHELLS
family Strombidae

Strombs (conches) and spider shells possess medium to large, thick shells, which are distinguished by the presence of the stromboid notch, a furrow towards the front end of the outer lip, through which the animal extends its stalked left eye. The shell may be smooth or ridged. Spider shells are so named because of the finger-like extensions of the aperture. Strombids inhabit intertidal and subtidal areas among sand, coral or mud, where they feed on algae and detritus. They possess a long, claw-like operculum, which is used to assist with locomotion.

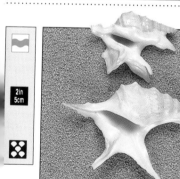

APORRHAIS PESPELICANI

AUTHORITY: (Linnaeus 1758)
COMMON NAME: Common pelican's foot
GENERAL DESCRIPTION: The aperture of the common pelican's foot is extended to produce four finger-like outgrowths, resembling a bird's foot, hence its common name. The whorls are angular and nodulose. The shells are usually cream coloured or off-white, although some may be darker brown. The species is widely distributed, being found from the Mediterranean to Norway, inhabiting deeper muddy offshore areas down to depths in excess of 450ft (140m).
DISTRIBUTION: Mediterranean; northwest Europe

LAMBIS LAMBIS

AUTHORITY: (Linnaeus 1758)
COMMON NAME: Common spider conch
GENERAL DESCRIPTION: This is one of the best known and most widely distributed species, with its finger-like extensions to the outer lip of the wide aperture. The shell of the female has longer spines and tends to be bigger; immature shells lack spines altogether. The larger of the shells illustrated is the rarer, orange form from west Australia. Usually, the shells are a creamy-white with orange-brown markings.
DISTRIBUTION: Indo-Pacific

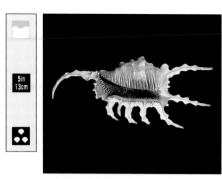

LAMBIS SCORPIUS SCORPIUS

AUTHORITY: (Linnaeus 1758)
COMMON NAME: Scorpion spider conch
GENERAL DESCRIPTION: This species, which is found on coral reefs, is popular with collectors, its irregular shape and striking coloration giving it a spectacular appearance. The nodular exterior is coarsely ribbed and is coloured in various shades of brown, while the deep purple inner lip is also strongly ribbed. The spines, which are slender and crimped, are closed and flat.
DISTRIBUTION: Western Pacific

STROMBUS GIGAS

AUTHORITY: Linnaeus 1758
COMMON NAME: Queen conch
GENERAL DESCRIPTION: This large, solid shell, reaches up to 9in (23cm) in length and with a wide, flaring lip. The aperture is coloured in the most delicate shades of pink, while the cream-coloured exterior is normally covered by a brownish periostracum. Immature shells do not have the flaring lip. It occurs in shallow water on sandy substrates. The species, which is edible, sometimes produces pink pearls. With the apex removed, it has been used as a form of trumpet.
DISTRIBUTION: South Florida; Caribbean

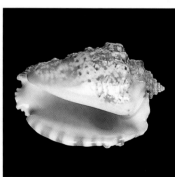

LAMBIS CHIRAGRA CHIRAGRA

AUTHORITY: (Linnaeus 1758)
COMMON NAME: Chiragra spider conch
GENERAL DESCRIPTION: This familiar species has a large, thick, heavy shell. There are five characteristic slightly curved, finger-like projections, and the siphonal canal extends from the base of the columella, giving rise to a "sixth", straight spine. The white body whorl has irregular, lumpy, spiral ridges and is spotted with brown. The aperture may be pink, yellow, red or brown. It occurs in shallow sandy areas and on coral reefs.
DISTRIBUTION: Indo-Pacific

STROMBUS LENTIGINOSUS

AUTHORITY: Linnaeus 1758
COMMON NAME: Silver conch
GENERAL DESCRIPTION: The silver conch has a solid shell with a short, pointed spire and a body whorl bearing blunt nodules. The outer expanded lip, which is thickened and reflexed, is patterned by approximately eight broad, greyish-brown bands. The upper surface is a creamy white, mottled with orange-brown streaks and blotches. It occurs on coral sand and down to about 12ft (4m).
DISTRIBUTION: Indo-Pacific

STROMBUS MUTABILIS

AUTHORITY: Swainson 1821
COMMON NAME: Mutable conch
GENERAL DESCRIPTION: This is, as its name implies, a highly variable species. It has a large angular body whorl and a short spire. Both the aperture and the columella are ridged. Colour variations abound, but the aperture is normally orange to pink, with fine striations. It occurs in sandy, coral areas down to about 60ft (20m).
DISTRIBUTION: Tropical Indo-Pacific

TROMBUS VOMER

THORITY: (Röding 1798)
MMON NAME: Vomer conch
NERAL DESCRIPTION: This slender shell, with its ɔular, coronated whorls and anterior finger-like extension ʰe aperture lip, is an uncommon species, much sought ʳ by collectors. The upper surface is a pale cream mottled ʰ reddish-brown, while the interior of the aperture is ınge. It occurs on sand in shallow water.
STRIBUTION: Southwest Pacific

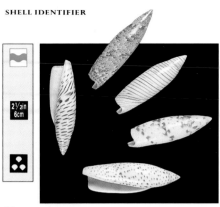

TEREBELLUM TEREBELLUM

AUTHORITY: (Linnaeus 1758)
COMMON NAME: Little auger shell
GENERAL DESCRIPTION: These slim, highly glossy shells are readily identified by their bullet-like appearance. Although it is a monotypic genus, the colour and pattern variations within the species differ considerably, as can be seen from the examples illustrated. All the shells have an enlarged body whorl and short, straight-sided spire. The aperture is narrow. They are widely distributed throughout the Indo-Pacific, inhabiting shallow-water, sandy bays.
DISTRIBUTION: Indo-Pacific

SUPER FAMILY

CREPIDULOIDEA

SLIPPER, CUP AND SAUCER SHELLS

family Crepidulidae

The slipper shells and cup-and-saucer limpets have a worldwide distribution. They have no operculum but possess either a shelf-like process or small internal cup to protect the animal's soft organs. They live on rocks or on the backs of other shelled creatures, where they filter-feed on vegetable matter.

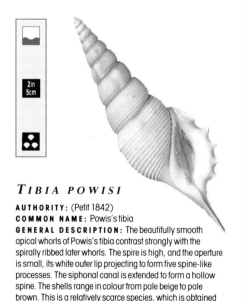

TIBIA POWISI

AUTHORITY: (Petit 1842)
COMMON NAME: Powis's tibia
GENERAL DESCRIPTION: The beautifully smooth apical whorls of Powis's tibia contrast strongly with the spirally ribbed later whorls. The spire is high, and the aperture is small, its white outer lip projecting to form five spine-like processes. The siphonal canal is extended to form a hollow spine. The shells range in colour from pale beige to pale brown. This is a relatively scarce species, which is obtained from moderately deep water by dredging.
DISTRIBUTION: Southwest Pacific to Australia

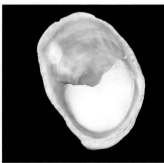

CREPIDULA FORNICATA

AUTHORITY: (Linnaeus 1758)
COMMON NAME: Common Atlantic slipper
GENERAL DESCRIPTION: The common Atlantic slipper inhabits the eastern United States and northeast Atlantic coasts, having been introduced to UK waters with oysters. The light brown, or pinkish-beige mottled shell is a flattened boat shape, and it has an extremely large body whorl. It may be either smooth or ridged. The aperture is partially closed by a white, shelf-like partition. It is a subtidal, rock-dwelling species, which lives in chain-like colonies.
DISTRIBUTION: Eastern United States; northwest Europe

SUPER FAMILY

XENOPHOROIDEA

CARRIER SHELLS

family Xenophoridae

Carrier shells of the genus *Xenophora* are among the most fascinating of all molluscan families and may, perhaps, be regarded as the true "original shell collectors" because most species cement sea-floor debris such as coral or shells to their own shells. It is not known if this bizarre behaviour is to provide a means of camouflage, to provide strength and rigidity, or simply to prevent the creatures from sinking into a muddy sub-strate. They possess a corneous operculum and inhabit tropical and warm seas.

SUPER FAMILY

CYPRAEOIDEA

COWRY SHELLS

family Cypraeidae

The Cypraeidae inhabit the tropical waters of the Indo-Pacific. They are among the most collectable and popular of all shells, being brightly coloured, glossy and smooth. The aperture of adult specimens is slit-like and generally "toothed", and it appears to be on the lower surface since the body whorl grows over and encases the shell spire. There are more than 200 different species, all of which are omnivorous, but there are numerous local variations in size and colour.

4in
10cm

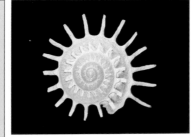

7½in
19cm

STELLARIA SOLARIS

UTHORITY: (Linnaeus 1758)

OMMON NAME: Sunburst carrier shell

ENERAL DESCRIPTION: The cream-coloured sunburst arrier shell is atypical of carrier shells since it does not sually ornament itself by cementing coral or shell material to s shell, although the apical whorls are covered with debris. It nakes up for this, however, by producing the radiating hollow pines that give it its spectacular outline. These spines touch ut are not attached to the underlying whorl. It occurs in the ndo-Pacific from just offshore down to considerable depths, nd it is unusual to find specimens in which the spines are erfect.

ISTRIBUTION: Indo-Pacific

CYPRAEA CERVUS

AUTHORITY: Linnaeus 1771

COMMON NAME: Atlantic deer cowry

GENERAL DESCRIPTION: The Atlantic deer cowry is the largest in the genus, but it has become scarce in recent years, possibly through over-collecting, and it is now unusual to find specimens larger than 6in (15cm). The shell itself is surprisingly light. It is a rich brown colour, with paler grey spots, which cease at the margins. There is a wide dorsal line. The interior is a pale lavender. The aperture bears prominent, dark brown teeth. It can be found from low-tide level to about 60ft (20m) and occurs in Bermuda and from North Carolina to Cuba.

DISTRIBUTION: North Carolina to Cuba; Bermuda

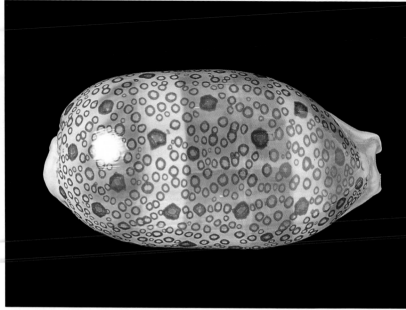

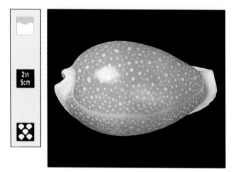

CYPRAEA MILIARIS

AUTHORITY: Gmelin 1791
COMMON NAME: Millet cowry
GENERAL DESCRIPTION: This shallow-water species, with its slightly humped dorsum, is relatively common throughout the west Pacific as well as off north Australia. The shell, a pale mustard yellow, is covered by small irregular spots. There is a clear dorsal line, and the base and margins are white. The aperture bears coarse teeth. It grows up to 2in (5cm) but average specimens measure just over 1in (2.5cm).
DISTRIBUTION: West Pacific; north Australia

CYPRAEA ARGUS

AUTHORITY: Linnaeus 1771
COMMON NAME: Eyed cowry
GENERAL DESCRIPTION: This is an unmistakable species. The upper surface of the parallel-sided shell is covered with irregular rings or "eyes" and dark brown blotches on a beige ground. The aperture, which is wider at the front than at the rear, is fringed with moderately coarse teeth. The base is pale brown with two distinctive dark bands. It inhabits coral reefs in the Indian Ocean and southwest Pacific, including Australia, but is uncommon.
DISTRIBUTION: Indian Ocean; southwest Pacific

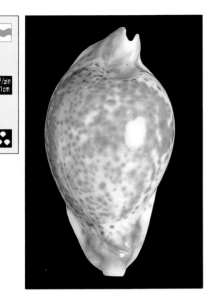

CYPRAEA HESITATA

AUTHORITY: Iredale 1916
COMMON NAME: Umbilicate cowry
GENERAL DESCRIPTION: This strikingly shaped cowry, with its humped dorsum and extended anterior and posterior canals, is found in several forms, and its taxonomic status is, therefore, uncertain. The shell is basically off-white, covered with light brown blotches. The teeth are short and quite fine. It occurs offshore in southeast Australia and was once considered rare; it is now trawled in fairly reasonable numbers, however.
DISTRIBUTION: Southeast Australia

EGG SHELLS

family Ovulidae

The false or egg cowries are similar in shape
to their close relations, the true cowries, but
they tend to have few or no apertural teeth.
They inhabit tropical seas, most being found
in Indo-Pacific waters, where they live
among colonial sponges, soft corals,
sea fans and gorgonian corals.

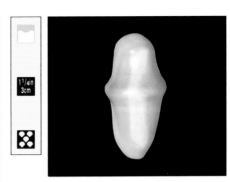

CYPHOMA GIBBOSUM

AUTHORITY: (Linnaeus 1758)
COMMON NAME: Flamingo tongue
GENERAL DESCRIPTION: The flamingo tongue occurs in shallow waters on sea whip and gorgonian corals from the southeast United States to Brazil as well as Bermuda. It is a relatively common species, which has a thick, rather solid shell with a central raised ridge. The shell is a pale apricot colour, and the aperture and base are creamy white. The aperture is devoid of teeth.
DISTRIBUTION: Southeastern United States to Brazil; Bermuda

OVULA OVUM

AUTHORITY: (Linnaeus 1758)
COMMON NAME: Common egg shell
GENERAL DESCRIPTION: This well-known shell, with its attractive, glossy white dorsum and orange-brown interior, occurs throughout the Indo-Pacific, including Australia, where it lives in shallow-water reefs among black sponges. The aperture curves smoothly over its entire length, and the lip is coarsely ridged on the underside. It is often used to decorate native canoes as well as being used for fish and octopus lures.
DISTRIBUTION: Indo-Pacific

ALLIED COWRIES
family Triviidae

Members of the Triviidae family resemble small cowries, but their shells are less glossy and are traversed by radial ridges. The animal has no operculum. The majority occur in the tropics and can be found beneath stones and rocks at low tide feeding on ascidians and sponges.

MOON OR NECKLACE SHELLS
family Naticidae

Moon or necklace shells are found throughout the world. The species are all carnivorous, feeding mainly on other molluscs and crustacea by rasping a circular hole in the shell of their prey by means of a file-like radula. The glossy shells range in size from small to medium, and they have short spires and large body whorls with large, semicircular apertures. The animal has an operculum and lives in sand or mud from the intertidal zone to deep water.

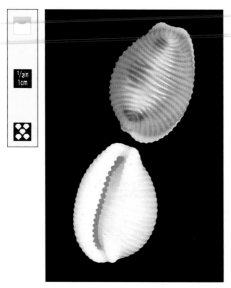

1/2in
1cm

TRIVIA MONACHA

AUTHORITY: (Da Costa 1778)
COMMON NAME: European cowry
GENERAL DESCRIPTION: The European cowry, which is also known as the bean cowry, has a small, solid shell, which is distinctly ribbed. The dorsal surface is pale beige or grey and bears three darker spots. The base is white. It inhabits the northeast Atlantic and Mediterranean where it is to be found feeding on encrusting sponge under rocks exposed at extreme low tide. The shells illustrated are from Portugal.
DISTRIBUTION: Northeast Atlantic; Mediterranean

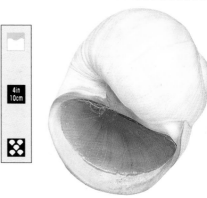

4in
10cm

EUSPIRA LEWISI

AUTHORITY: (Gould 1847)
COMMON NAME: Lewis's moon
GENERAL DESCRIPTION: This is the largest species in the family, and specimens can grow to 4in (10cm) in length. It has a thick, heavy, chalky white shell, but the interior and lip are pale brown. There is an open umbilicus. It lives in sandy areas and can be found in the intertidal zone and subtidal waters. The specimen shown here was collected in Puget Sound, Washington.
DISTRIBUTION: British Columbia to Baja California

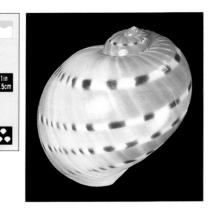

...ATICA ALAPAPILIONIS

...THORITY: (Röding 1798)
...MMON NAME: Butterfly moon
...NERAL DESCRIPTION: The butterfly moon has a tiny ...re and a large, globose body whorl, which is decorated by ...r distinct spiral rows of brown dashes on a pale beige ...ckground. The aperture and surrounding area are white. ...e shell illustrated was obtained from off Thailand.
...STRIBUTION: Indo-Pacific

> SUPER FAMILY
> TONNOIDEA

TUN SHELLS
family Tonnidae
Tuns or cask shells comprise a small family, but the shells are medium to large. The thin, globose shells have short spires and inflated body whorls, which are spirally corded and covered by a thin periostracum. The aperture is expanded and normally has a crenulate outer lip. The umbilicus is deep and there is no operculum. They are mainly tropical creatures, inhabiting deep water where they feed carnivorously on fish, sea urchins, sea cucumbers and crustacea.

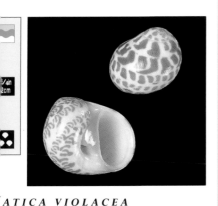

...ATICA VIOLACEA

...THORITY: Sowerby 1825
...MMON NAME: Violet moon
...NERAL DESCRIPTION: The distinctive violet and tan ...oration has made this shell extremely popular with ...ectors. It has a globose body whorl, a rounded spire and a ...all umbilicus. The aperture is white. It may be found in ...allow water down to about 70ft (21m) and the shells ...wn here were collected from Kwajalein Atoll in the ...rshall Islands in the western Pacific Ocean.
...STRIBUTION: Indo-Pacific

TONNA SULCOSA

AUTHORITY: (Born 1778)
COMMON NAME: Banded tun
GENERAL DESCRIPTION: The brown banding on the cream background has given this species its common name. The apex is a darker, purple colour. The lower edge of the aperture is dentate, and there is a deep siphonal canal. Live examples are covered with a dark brown periostracum. The specimen shown here was obtained in the central Philippines.
DISTRIBUTION: Indo-Pacific

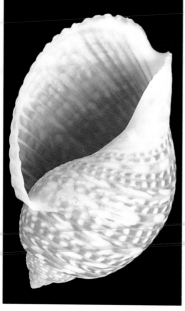

FIG SHELLS

family Ficidae

These shells get their name from their characteristic shape, reminiscent of figs, with a short spire enveloped in the large, inflated body whorl. The thin outer lip is curved, and there is an elongated siphonal canal. The shell surface is crossed by a series of raised vertical and spiral ridges to form a reticulate decoration. There is no operculum. They inhabit tropical seas, occurring in sand or rubble from shallow to deep water, where they feed on sea urchins and other echinoderms.

TONNA PERDIX

AUTHORITY: (Linnaeus 1758)
COMMON NAME: Partridge tun
GENERAL DESCRIPTION: The high, pointed spire readily distinguishes this species from other tuns. The body whorl bears flattened spiral ribbing and is cream with a series of brown squares and dashes. The outer lip is thickened but not crenulate. The name is said to derive from the resemblance of the shell's coloration to the plumage of the European partridge. The shell, although large, is comparatively fragile. It is found offshore in sandy areas throughout Indo-Pacific waters.
DISTRIBUTION: Indo-Pacific

FICUS SUBINTERMEDIA

AUTHORITY: (Orbigny 1852)
COMMON NAME: Underlined fig
GENERAL DESCRIPTION: This is one of the more robust members of the group. The coarse reticulate decoration, in medium to dark brown, contrasts with the four or five cream spiral bands, which enclose darker spots. The aperture runs almost the whole length of the body whorl. The interior is usually a pale mauve, although it is sometimes greyish-brown. It occurs in shallow water with sand or mud bottoms.
DISTRIBUTION: Indo-Pacific

HELMET OR BONNET SHELLS

family Cassidae

This is a large family, containing some 80 living species. Helmet or bonnet shells are medium to large in size, solid and often heavy. They have a short spire and an inflated body whorl, which may be sculptured by a series of nodular ribs. The aperture is long and often has a thickened, toothed outer lip, which may be expanded. The operculum is thin, semicircular and horny. Helmet shells prefer warmer seas, where they burrow into sand from the intertidal zone to deep water. They feed on echinoderms.

CYPRAECASSIS RUFA

AUTHORITY: (Linnaeus 1758)
COMMON NAME: Bullmouth helmet
GENERAL DESCRIPTION: This thick, solid, heavy, reddish-brown shell is often known as the cameo shell. Large quantities are exported from Africa to Italy to be used in the manufacture of cameos, which are produced by selective carving of the different shell layers. The present industry began about 150 years ago. The spire is low, and the aperture large. The shell has rounded dorsal nodules, and the lip is thick and dentate. It is found near coral reefs.
DISTRIBUTION: Indo-Pacific

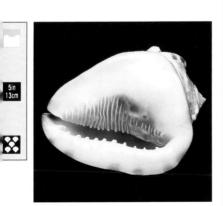

CASSIS FLAMMEA

AUTHORITY: (Linnaeus 1758)
COMMON NAME: Flame helmet
GENERAL DESCRIPTION: This shallow-water dweller is a low spire and a nodulose body whorl, especially on the boulders. The cream-coloured aperture has a triangular outline, and the outer lip has a series of dark blotches. The main body whorl is cream coloured, mottled with light and dark brown. The siphonal canal is twisted and upturned.
DISTRIBUTION: Bermuda; Florida; Caribbean

PHALIUM AREOLA

AUTHORITY: (Linnaeus 1758)
COMMON NAME: Chequered bonnet
GENERAL DESCRIPTION: This attractive ovate shell has a smooth, glossy surface, which is decorated with a series of rich orange-brown squares. The spire is medium sized and has several raised varices. The apertural lip is thin and folded, and there are about 20 sharp teeth on the outer edge. It occurs in sandy mud in intertidal and offshore waters.
DISTRIBUTION: West Indo-Pacific

THE TRITONS
family Ranellidae

Tritons have small to large, solid shells with strong varices, spiral cords and nodular sculpture. Living specimens are covered in a thick, often hairy, periostracum. The outer lip is thickened and is often toothed or crenulate. The columella is plicate, while the operculum is thick and horny. Tritons have a wide distribution, possibly because some species produce free-swimming veliger larvae, which can survive for over three months. They occur on coral and rocky reefs from intertidal to deep water, feeding on sea urchins and molluscs.

CHARONIA TRITONIS

AUTHORITY: (Linnaeus 1758)
COMMON NAME: Trumpet triton
GENERAL DESCRIPTION: This is the largest and best known species in the family, with its tall, elegant spire, rounded whorls and distinctive coloration. The aperture is a deep orange, and the large lip has white channels between the teeth on the outer edge. As its common name suggests, it has often been used as a trumpet by drilling a hole near the apex into which a mouthpiece is then inserted. It occurs on coral reefs in shallow water.
DISTRIBUTION: Indo-Pacific

RANELLA OLEARIUM

AUTHORITY: (Linnaeus 1758)
COMMON NAME: Wandering triton
GENERAL DESCRIPTION: This is one of the most widely distributed species, as its common name implies. Although the shells vary considerably in size, thickness and colour, the constant shape, rounded body whorl and tall spire with a pair of oblique varices down each side, make them easy to identify. The aperture is almost round, with a small canal at the top, and there are approximately 17 teeth on the outer lip. This shell was obtained from deep water off southeast Italy.
DISTRIBUTION: Caribbean; Mediterranean; Africa; Australia; New Zealand

CYMATIUM PARTHENOPEUM

AUTHORITY: (Von Salis 1793)
COMMON NAME: Neapolitan triton
GENERAL DESCRIPTION: Another widely dispersed species, the Neapolitan triton has a solidly built shell with heavily corded whorls and a medium spire. The wide aperture has six teeth on its thickened outer lip and a ridged columella wall. It occurs offshore down to a depth of over 200ft (60m). Live examples have a densely bristled periostracum, which masks the pale brown shell with its darker brown varices and aperture. The specimen shown here is from southeast Africa, but the species is found in warm seas throughout the world.
DISTRIBUTION: Worldwide in tropical and warm seas

FROG SHELLS
family Bursidae

Frog shells are superficially very like tritons, but they may be distinguished by the short, distinct groove at the upper corner of the aperture. The shell is thick and heavy, with angular whorls sculptured by nodules and varices. The outer lip is thick and crenulate. The operculum is thick and horny and has a marginal nucleus. They live in sand or mud or on coral or rocky reefs in shallow water, feeding on marine worms.

SUPER FAMILY
EPITONIOIDEA

WENTLETRAPS
family Epitoniidae

Wentletraps are found throughout the world, and there are about 200 living species of these exquisitely ornamented shells. The small to medium-sized shells are often loosely coiled and decorated by prominent axial varices or cancellate sculpture, and the common name derives from the Dutch word for a spiral staircase. The circular aperture has a thickened lip, and the operculum is horny. Wentletraps occur in shallow to deep water, feeding on corals and sea anemones.

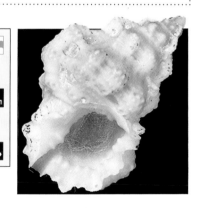

1 in
2.5cm

2¹/₂in
6cm

EPITONIUM SCALARE

AUTHORITY: (Linnaeus 1758)
COMMON NAME: Precious wentletrap
GENERAL DESCRIPTION: Once considered rare and greatly coveted, this species has recently been obtained in relatively large numbers by dredging off Taiwan and the Philippines. The large, openly coiled shell is white or cream in colour. The loose, rounded whorls are separated by strong, blade-like varices, which are connected to each other at the open suture. The wide umbilicus is open. It occurs from extreme low water downwards to about 100ft (30m). Tradition has it that this species was so rare that the Chinese produced replicas of it in rice paste in the 18th century.
DISTRIBUTION: Japan to southwest Pacific

BURSA THOMAE

AUTHORITY: (Orbigny 1842)
COMMON NAME: St Thomas frog shell
GENERAL DESCRIPTION: This is a small species. There are a few nodular whorls, and the varices are aligned. The lips are crenulate, and the pale lavender colour of the aperture contrasts with the overall pale beige of the shell body. A fairly common shell, it lives on or under rocks down about 250ft (75m).
DISTRIBUTION: South Carolina to Brazil; Cape Verde Islands

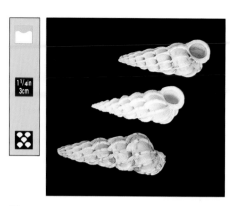

EPITONIUM CLATHRUM

AUTHORITY: (Linnaeus 1758)
COMMON NAME: Common European wentletrap
GENERAL DESCRIPTION: Dead shells are often found in shell debris among rocks on the southern coasts of the UK. It is a small, narrow but robust shell, with many suture-joined varices, which hold together the rounded whorls. The colours vary from white to tan, traversed by a series of fine brown spiral bands, particularly evident on the varices.
DISTRIBUTION: Northeast Atlantic; Mediterranean

JANTHINA JANTHINA

AUTHORITY: (Linnaeus 1758)
COMMON NAME: Common janthina
GENERAL DESCRIPTION: This, the largest member of the family, exhibits considerable variation in shell shape, but because it is so difficult to observe these animals in the "field", the reason for this variation is unclear. Some shells have a low, rounded spire, while others have a medium spire with almost flat-sided whorls. The body whorl, however, is always large and inflated. After severe storms shells periodically get washed up on shores worldwide, from the UK to Australia. The examples illustrated are from northern Queensland.
DISTRIBUTION: Worldwide in tropical seas

PURPLE SEA SNAILS

family Janthinidae

The distinctive violet coloration of members of this family gives them their common name, and also makes them popular with collectors. The small to medium-sized shells are thin and fragile. The inflated body whorl, expanded aperture and absence of an operculum are suited to the pelagic existence of these sea snails, which float upside down on the ocean surface by means of a "raft", composed of mucus-enveloped air bubbles, feeding on pelagic jellyfish and mollusc larvae.

SUPER FAMILY

MURICOIDEA

ROCK SHELLS

family Muricidae

There are more than 1,000 species of rock shell distributed worldwide, and they range in size from small to large. They have high, pointed spires, and the siphonal canal may be extended as a long spiny process. The oval aperture may have dentate lips. There is a thick, horny operculum. The whorls may be smooth, nodular or spiny, or they may have strong varices. Rock shells occur on rocks, coral, sand or mud from intertidal to deep subtidal, where they feed on molluscs, barnacles, corals and marine worms.

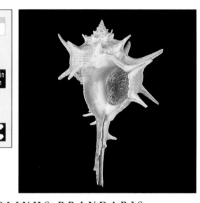

3¹/₂in 9cm

BOLINUS BRANDARIS

AUTHORITY: (Linnaeus 1758)
COMMON NAME: Purple dye murex
GENERAL DESCRIPTION: This well-known Mediterranean species is one of the two shellfish used in Roman times in the production of the purple dye, Tyrian purple. The club-shaped shell varies in sculpture, and there may or may not be spines. It is generally pale brown with a richer brown interior. It occurs in sandy areas in shallow subtidal waters.
DISTRIBUTION: Mediterranean; northwest Africa

3in 7.5cm

HEXAPLEX TRUNCULUS

AUTHORITY: (Linnaeus 1758)
COMMON NAME: Trunculus murex
GENERAL DESCRIPTION: This species, sometimes known as the trunk murex, is confined to the Mediterranean and is the other species used in the production of Tyrian purple. The two specimens shown here illustrate the variations in shape that can occur, but the colour of the banded shades of brown is fairly constant. The body whorl is large, and the spire is pointed. It is readily distinguished from *Bolinus brandaris* by its short, broad siphonal canal.
DISTRIBUTION: Mediterranean

6in 15cm

HAUSTELLUM HAUSTELLUM

AUTHORITY: (Linnaeus 1758)
COMMON NAME: Snipe's bill murex
GENERAL DESCRIPTION: The distinctive shape gives this species its common name – the side view is thought to resemble a bird's head. This is the largest species in its genus, and it is a low-spired, solid shell. There is a bulbous, enlarged body whorl, with a long, straight siphonal canal, which may be recurved at the anterior. The whorls are decorated with fine spiral cords and low, rounded nodules. The shell is coloured in various shades of brown, which contrast markedly with the pink aperture. It can be found in shallow water.
DISTRIBUTION: Indo-Pacific

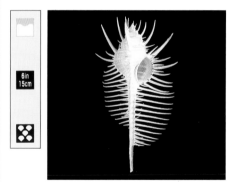

6in 15cm

MUREX PECTEN

AUTHORITY: Lightfoot 1786
COMMON NAME: Venus comb murex
GENERAL DESCRIPTION: This is one of the most attractive of the spiny murexes. Its long, often curved spines look so fragile that it is amazing that these exquisite shells can survive intact. The whorls are rounded and bulbous and bear many spiral cords. The shell is pale beige to mid-brown, but the aperture is white. It occurs in sandy offshore areas. The shell illustrated came from the central Philippines.
DISTRIBUTION: Indo-Pacific

DRUPA MORUM

AUTHORITY: Röding 1798
COMMON NAME: Purple drupe
GENERAL DESCRIPTION: This species is easily recognized by its flat spire, large, nodular body whorl and purple aperture, which is strongly dentate. The outer lip of the aperture extends to form spines. It is whitish-grey with black nodules. This is a relatively common shell, which can be found on most tropical, intertidal coral reefs, feeding on small invertebrates.
DISTRIBUTION: Indo-Pacific

PURPURA PATULA

AUTHORITY: (Linnaeus 1758)
COMMON NAME: Wide-mouthed purpura
GENERAL DESCRIPTION: This well-known shell has a large body whorl and a relatively small spire. The aperture is large, and the outer lip is slightly toothed. The exterior is sculptured with rows of blunt nodules and fine cords. The dull grey-brown exterior contrasts with the rich orange columella and greyish-white interior. It occurs on intertidal rocky cliffs. This species is still used by Central American Indians as a source of dye.
DISTRIBUTION: Southeast Florida; West Indies

OCINEBRA ERINACEUS

AUTHORITY: (Linnaeus 1758)
COMMON NAME: Sting winkle
GENERAL DESCRIPTION: The oyster drill or common sting winkle is a very variable shell. It has a pointed apex and large body whorl, with up to nine varices, covered with fluted scales. The colour varies through shades of brown, but the aperture is normally white. It occurs in subtidal areas, where it feeds on bivalves, and it is considered a pest in oyster beds.
DISTRIBUTION: Northwest Europe to west Africa

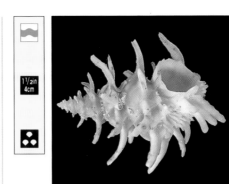

NUCELLA LAPILLUS

AUTHORITY: (Linnaeus 1758)
COMMON NAME: Atlantic dog whelk
GENERAL DESCRIPTION: The sturdy shell of this species is highly suitable for life on the wave-swept rocky shores of the Atlantic coasts. The shell may be smooth or covered by regularly placed, distinct, frill-like ribs. It feeds on barnacles and other molluscs, and the considerable variation in colour and banding seen in these specimens from Cornwall, UK, may be caused by differences in its prey.
DISTRIBUTION: Northeast United States; west Europe

BABELOMUREX SPINOSUS

AUTHORITY: (Hirase 1908)
COMMON NAME: Spined latiaxis
GENERAL DESCRIPTION: The spined latiaxis well deserves its common name, as can be seen from the specimen illustrated here, which was collected off southwest Taiwan. These delicate shells are off-white, cream or pale brown. They have a tall spire, angular whorls and a short, narrow, recurved canal. They are found in subtidal, offshore waters.
DISTRIBUTION: Japan to Philippines; Australia

LATIAXIS SHELLS

family Coralliophilidae

Latiaxis shells, with their exquisite shapes and delicate coloration, are greatly prized by collectors. The shells vary in size and shape, with short or long siphonal canals. The whorls may be smooth or covered with spines, but a brown, horny operculum is normally present. They differ from rock shells in not having a radula. They live in shallow to deep water, feeding on corals and sea anemones.

BABELOMUREX LISCHKEANUS

AUTHORITY: (Dunker 1882)
COMMON NAME: Lischke's latiaxis
GENERAL DESCRIPTION: This widespread species, with its pagoda-like outline, may vary from place to place, but the true beauty of its highly spinose spiral ridges and large, triangular shoulder spines cannot be fully appreciated until they are seen under a hand lens. The shells inhabit relatively deep water; the specimen illustrated was fished off Taiwan.
DISTRIBUTION: Japan; Philippines; Australia; New Zealand

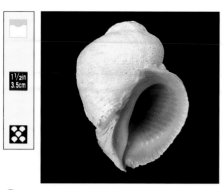

CORALLIOPHILA VIOLACEA

AUTHORITY: (Kiener 1836)
COMMON NAME: Violet coral snail
GENERAL DESCRIPTION: This globose shell, with its large body whorl and low spire, is normally heavily encrusted, which makes it difficult to see as it shelters under coral. Fine spinal cords are visible on exposed parts. The deep purple aperture with its delicate spiral ridges is characteristic. This example was obtained from the central Philippines.
DISTRIBUTION: Indo-Pacific

WHELKS
family Buccinidae
Members of the whelk family have small to large globose shells with tapered spires. The aperture is expanded and smooth and often has a thickened outer lip. The whorls are smooth or sculptured with radial ribs and spiral cords. The siphonal canal varies from short to long, and a thin, horny, brown operculum is present. They occur among rocks, coral or in sand from the intertidal area to deep cold water, feeding on bivalves, worms and carrion.

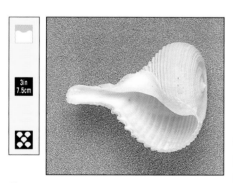

RAPA RAPA

AUTHORITY: (Linnaeus 1758)
COMMON NAME: Bubble turnip
GENERAL DESCRIPTION: This whelk is the largest of the turnips. It has a thin, fragile but large and globose shell with a short spire and a pointed apex that is almost lost in the body whorl. It lives embedded in the soft corals on which it feeds. It is normally a uniform white, but occasional orange forms occur. The aperture is always white. The whorls are decorated by spiral shell ribbing. The animal's thin, horny operculum is too small to be an effective closure for the aperture.
DISTRIBUTION: Southwest Pacific

BUCCINUM UNDATUM

AUTHORITY: Linnaeus 1758
COMMON NAME: Edible European whelk
GENERAL DESCRIPTION: This well-known species, sometimes known as the common northern whelk, has been used for food for centuries. It lives at various depths, from shallow to deep water. It is variable in shape, but is normally grey-brown in colour. Live shells are covered by a greenish-brown periostracum. It feeds chiefly on carrion and often comes up in crab-pots. Left-handed examples occasionally occur.
DISTRIBUTION: Northeast United States; west Europe

NEPTUNEA TABULATA

AUTHORITY: (Baird 1863)
COMMON NAME: Tabled neptune
GENERAL DESCRIPTION: The distinctive, shelf-like, shouldered whorls readily identify this deep-water species, which lives at depths around 1,300ft (400m). It is a uniform yellowish-white in colour. The spire is high, and the body whorl is long. The elongated aperture has a sharp-edged outer lip.
DISTRIBUTION: West Canada to California

DOVE SHELLS
family Columbellidae
This large family of mainly small, smooth, solid and brightly coloured shells occurs in intertidal to deep waters of warm and tropical seas. The shell aperture is long and thickened with a denticulate outer lip. The whorls are smooth or have axial and spiral ribbing. A long, horny operculum is normally present. They can be found beneath rocks or on sand, mud or seaweeds, scavenging on animal matter. The family contains over 400 species.

PHOS SENTICOSUS

AUTHORITY: (Linnaeus 1758)
COMMON NAME: Phos whelk
GENERAL DESCRIPTION: This attractive little species, which is also sometimes known as the thorny thos, can be found in tropical tidal sand and mud flats down to about 30ft (10m). The strong axial ribs are spinose where they are crossed by spiral cords. The siphonal canal is short, and there are up to four indistinct ridges at the base of the columella. Specimens vary in colour from cream to brown, and they may be banded. The aperture may be white or lavender.
DISTRIBUTION: Indo-Pacific

COLUMBELLA MERCATORIA

AUTHORITY: (Linnaeus 1758)
COMMON NAME: Common dove shell
GENERAL DESCRIPTION: The apex of this small, solid species is often missing. The spire is fairly short, and the body whorl, which is large, is sculptured by a series of fine spiral cords. The aperture has a dentate outer lip and a ridged columella. The shell is white, mottled by variable orange or brown patches. It occurs under rocks in shallow water, the shells illustrated being from Yucatan, Mexico.
DISTRIBUTION: Florida to Brazil; Bermuda

DOG WHELKS
family Nassariidae
The large family of dog whelks or nassa mud snails consists of small, solid and ovate shells, which are often strongly nodular. The rounded aperture is notched at its base. The columella has a marked callus deposit, and the small, horny operculum has a serrated edge. The shells commonly occur on intertidal sands and mud flats, although some species live on sand or coral in subtidal waters. They are active scavengers, feeding on dead molluscs and other carrion.

CROWN AND SWAMP CONCHES
family Melongenidae
This family includes the giant whelks, and, as this common name implies, includes medium to very large, solid shells of variable shape. The body whorl is inflated and often nodular or spinose at the shoulder. The expanded aperture has a smooth columella. The operculum is thick and horny. Giant whelks are commonly found on sand and mud flats or in subtidal waters, where they feed on bivalves and carrion.

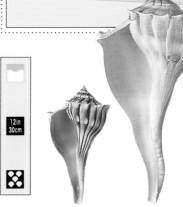

NASSARIUS PULLUS
AUTHORITY: (Linnaeus 1758)
COMMON NAME: Black nassa
GENERAL DESCRIPTION: The whorls of this small shell, with its cream-coloured parietal callus, are sculptured by a series of fine axial ribs, which are crossed by several radial cords. It is pale grey to brown in colour and often has brown spiral bands. The glazed parietal area and columella are a rich cream colour. It inhabits mud flats.
DISTRIBUTION: Indo-Pacific

BUSYCON CONTRARIUM
AUTHORITY: (Conrad 1840)
COMMON NAME: Lightning or left-handed whelk
GENERAL DESCRIPTION: This shell may be easily recognized by its naturally sinistral or left-handed coiling, although right-handed examples sometimes occur. It has a low spire and an enlarged body whorl, and the whorls are often spinose at the shoulder. Young shells are usually more distinctly coloured, with dark streaks traversing the surface. These streaks, which are reputed to represent lightning, are ill-defined in the more uniform beige colour of very large shells. It is common subtidally down to 100ft (30m) in sand.
DISTRIBUTION: Southeast United States

MELONGENA CORONA

AUTHORITY: (Gmelin 1791)
COMMON NAME: Florida crown conch
GENERAL DESCRIPTION: It exhibits considerable variation in form and colour. This diversity may be caused because the young develop directly in the egg capsule to emerge as miniature adults capable of crawling only short distances. As a result, populations become isolated and develop their own local characteristics. The basic colour is cream with spiral bands of grey, brown or orange. There are fine axial striations and coarse, strong growth lines. A single broken spiral ridge appears on lower part of body whorl.
DISTRIBUTION: Florida to northeastern Mexico

TULIP SHELLS

family Fasciolariidae

This large group, also known as spindle shells, contains medium to large, high-spired shells, which are often sculptured by nodules and spiral cords. The aperture is oval, and the columella is often ridged. The live shell is covered by a brown periostracum, and there is an oval, horny operculum. Tulip shells occur on sand or coral reefs from intertidal to deep water, and they feed on worms, bivalve molluscs or carrion.

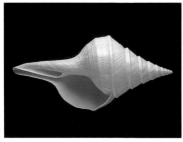

SYRINX ARUANUS

AUTHORITY: (Linnaeus 1758)
COMMON NAME: Australian trumpet
GENERAL DESCRIPTION: This is probably the largest living marine gastropod, which may achieve lengths of 30in (75cm). Its rich orange-brown colour is hidden in live samples by the thick, coarse, brown periostracum. The damaged apex of adult shells results from the breaking off of the large embryonic shell or protoconch. The body whorl is large, and all the whorls bear weak spiral ribs of varying depths. It occurs from low tide down to 30ft (10m). This species has been over-collected in recent years and is now protected by Australian law.
DISTRIBUTION: North Australia

FASCIOLARIA LILIUM HUNTERIA

AUTHORITY: (Perry 1811)
COMMON NAME: Banded tulip
GENERAL DESCRIPTION: The distinctive brown spiral banding, the rounded apex and smooth whorls make this an easily identified species. The shell is dull grey with yellowish streaks, or a yellowish-beige. There is no ridging or beading of the suture. It has an ovate, horny operculum, as can be seen in the illustration of a specimen from Florida. It occurs from the intertidal area down to depths of around 40ft (12m).
DISTRIBUTION: North Carolina to Texas

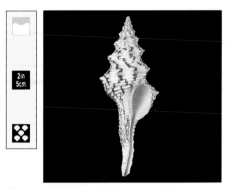

FUSINUS NICOBARICUS

AUTHORITY: (Röding 1798)
COMMON NAME: Nicobar spindle
GENERAL DESCRIPTION: This relatively small, stocky spindle has coarsely sculptured whorls with nodular shoulders and strong spiral ribbing. The body whorl has a secondary spiral rib. It is generally off-white, decorated with irregular brown patches. The aperture is white, and there are teeth inside the outer lip. The illustrated example was obtained off southeast India.
DISTRIBUTION: Indo-Pacific

THE VOLUTES

family Volutidae

The volutes are a large and highly collectable family of medium to large shells. Most species are coloured and patterned, and they have a narrow or expanded aperture, a ridged columella and generally smooth sculpture. Some species possess an operculum. They chiefly occur around the coasts of Australia, in shallow subtidal waters, buried in sand, mud or rubble, and they feed carnivorously on bivalves, gastropods or crustacea.

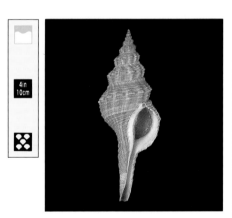

FUSINUS AUSTRALIS

AUTHORITY: (Quoy and Gaimard 1833)
COMMON NAME: Australian spindle
GENERAL DESCRIPTION: The angular whorls of this attractive uniform orange-brown species are sculpted by strong spiral cords. The shoulders are covered with fine tubercule-like projections. It has a horny operculum, and the aperture is white. It occurs in shallow water.
DISTRIBUTION: Southern and western Australia

LIVONIA MAMMILLA

AUTHORITY: (Sowerby 1844)
COMMON NAME: Mammal volute
GENERAL DESCRIPTION: Also known as the false melo volute. The shell is generally pale orange or cream marked by irregular brown squiggles, and the penultimate whorl is a darker brown. The aperture is wide, and the lip is expanded and flaring to reveal the rich orange interior. This species is native to southeastern Australia, where it occurs in deep water at depths around 650ft (200m).
DISTRIBUTION: Southeastern Australia

MELO AMPHORA

AUTHORITY: (Lightfoot 1786)
COMMON NAME: Australian baler
GENERAL DESCRIPTION: This is the largest species in the family and may reach sizes up to 15in (38cm). The common name derives from its having been used for baling out canoes by Aborigines and islanders of the Torres Straits. In recent years numerous examples have been caught by Taiwanese fishermen, and it is now often easier to obtain specimens from Taiwan than from their native Australia.
DISTRIBUTION: Tropical Australia; Papua New Guinea

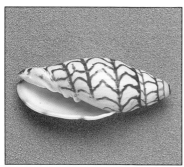

VOLUTOCONUS BEDNALLI

AUTHORITY: (Brazier 1878)
COMMON NAME: Bednall's volute
GENERAL DESCRIPTION: The distinctive dark brown, lattice-like markings over a cream-coloured base make this one of the most striking of all volutes, and this handsome species still commands high prices among collectors. The extended body whorl accounts for more than half the length, and the aperture is long, revealing the pale pink interior. The shell is native to the Northern Territory, where it prefers sandy areas at depths from between 30 and 300 feet (10–100m).
DISTRIBUTION: Northwest Australia

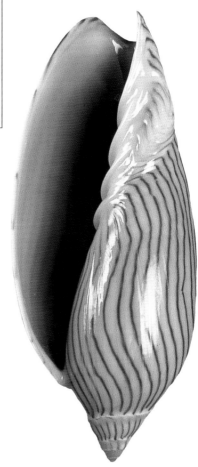

AMORIA ELLIOTI

AUTHORITY: (Sowerby 1864)
COMMON NAME: Elliot's volute
GENERAL DESCRIPTION: Elliot's volute is another handsome volute that is native to northwestern Australia. Its smooth, glossy appearance has made it a collector's favourite since its initial description well over 100 years ago. The spire is low, and the large body whorl tapers slightly at the anterior. This overall shape, combined with the distinctive, undulating dark brown markings on a cream background, contrasting with the rich brown interior, make it an easy species to identify.
DISTRIBUTION: Northwest Australia

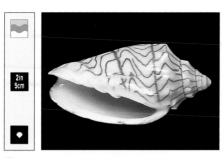

PARAMORIA GUNTHERI

AUTHORITY: (E. A. Smith 1886)
COMMON NAME: Gunther's volute
GENERAL DESCRIPTION: To own a Gunther's volute is a collector's dream — its beautiful chocolate brown undulating lines, crossed by two spiral bands of the same colour on a background of pinkish-cream present an exquisite picture. The margins of the aperture are cream, as is the columella. The interior is pale peach. The species is restricted to southern Australia, and the fortunate collector who found this example on a granite reef at a depth of just over 50ft (16m) off Memory Cove, Thorny Passage, must have been elated, since it normally occurs at depths of 130–260ft (40–80m).
DISTRIBUTION: Southern Australia

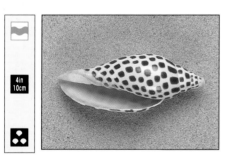

SCAPHELLA JUNONIA

AUTHORITY: (Lamarck 1804)
COMMON NAME: Juno's volute
GENERAL DESCRIPTION: This species, also sometimes known as the junonia, is also greatly prized by collectors. The almost straight-sided body whorl is patterned by striking dark brown squares on a white background. Its overall shape is fusiform, with a long, tapering body whorl and a moderate spire. The long aperture reveals a creamy-pink interior, on which the brown blotches of the exterior may be seen. It is a rare species, since it is rarely cast ashore, although it is fairly plentiful at depths of between 50 and 250 feet (15–75m) offshore.
DISTRIBUTION: Southeastern United States

HARP SHELLS

family Harpidae

Harp shells are carnivores with a worldwide distribution. Most of the species inhabit shallow waters, but some are found at depths of over 600ft (180m). There are 14 living species. They chiefly feed on crustacea, which they entrap in a film of mucus and sand before devouring. The shell has strong axial ribs, a wide aperture and smooth columella. There is no operculum.

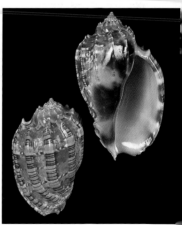

HARPA HARPA

AUTHORITY: (Linnaeus 1758)
COMMON NAME: True harp
GENERAL DESCRIPTION: The true harp or noble harp is common on sandy mud in deep water throughout Indo-Pacific waters and extending to the Great Barrier Reef of Australia. This species is variable in colour, but the low spire and the ribs, which can be broad or narrow, with the characteristic black lines, are typical. The shoulders bear sharp spines. The harp shells get their name from the smooth ribs, which are regularly spaced around the shell whorls, supposedly resembling the strings of a harp.
DISTRIBUTION: Indo-Pacific

VASE SHELLS

family Vasidae

Vase or chank shells belong to a small family with about 25 living species, which inhabit tropical coral reefs. The heavy, rather thick shells have from three to five strong spiral ridges on the columella, and they may be ornamented with short or long spines. They are carnivorous, feeding on worms and small bivalves, and possess a chitinous operculum.

PAGODA SHELLS

family Vasidae

Pagoda shells are considered here as a subfamily of the Vasidae. Some authorities regard them as a distinct family, Columbariidae. There are about 30 of these deep-water species, and they occur in tropical waters throughout the world. These small shells are characterized by the long siphonal canal and spines on the whorl shoulders. The animal has a chitinous operculum.

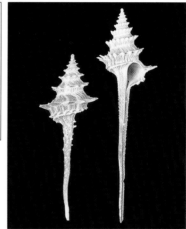

...LTIVASUM FLINDERSI

...THORITY: (Verco 1914)

...MMON NAME: Flinder's vase

...NERAL DESCRIPTION: Flinder's vase or chank shell ...nes from deep, offshore waters of southern and western ...tralia, and it is possibly the largest species of vase, ...wing to over 6in (15cm). The spire is tall, and the body ...orl is about the same length. The colour is variable, ...ging from white, through peach to a deep orange. The ...rture is small, and the thin outer lip has a wavy edge. ...larger of the shells illustrated is from west Australia; the ...aller one is from Coffin's Bay, south Australia.

...STRIBUTION: South and west Australia

COLUMBARIUM SPINICINCTUM

AUTHORITY: (Von Marténs 1881)

COMMON NAME: Spiny pagoda shell

GENERAL DESCRIPTION: The delicate, lightweight spiny pagoda shell is uncommon. It is found in east Australia, being most commonly dredged at depths of around 300ft (90m) off Queensland. The shells are beige, and are decorated with fine brown lines. The whorls are angular and are adorned with a central row of sharp, spiral, triangular spines. The long, narrow canal is also weakly spinose.

DISTRIBUTION: Eastern Australia

OLIVE SHELLS

family Olividae

These small to medium-sized cylindrical shells have a distinct posterior siphonal notch. The columella is often callused and sometimes has definite plicate ridges. The genus *Oliva* does not have an operculum, although some other members of the family have a thin, horny operculum. They occur in intertidal to deep water, burrowing through sand and mud in search of the small bivalves and crustacea on which they mainly feed.

OLIVA PORPHYRIA

AUTHORITY: (Linnaeus 1758)
COMMON NAME: Tent olive
GENERAL DESCRIPTION: This handsome shell is the largest member of the genus. It has a low spire with a sharp apical whorl and the large body whorl is rather long and swollen. The columella has definite plications. The background pale pinkish-violet colour is overlaid with the rich brown markings, said to resemble tents, from which the shell's common name is derived. In common with other members of the family, this species tends to remain hidden by burrowing in the sand during daylight, emerging only at night in search of food. It occurs in sand from the intertidal zone down to over 60ft (20m).
DISTRIBUTION: Gulf of California to Panama

3¹/₂ in
9cm

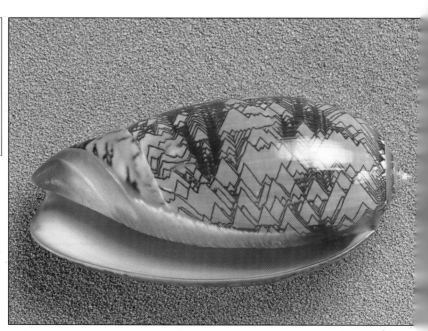

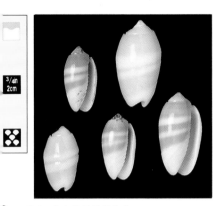

OLIVA CARNEOLA

AUTHORITY: (Gmelin 1791)
COMMON NAME: Carnelian olive
GENERAL DESCRIPTION: This is an extremely variable species that is, nevertheless, easily recognized. The distinctive little white shell is marked with two bands of varying colour. It is common on sand in shallow water, and as often used by islanders to produce necklaces or other ornamental decorations.
DISTRIBUTION: Tropical Indo-Pacific

OLIVA AUSTRALIS

AUTHORITY: Duclos 1835
COMMON NAME: Australian olive
GENERAL DESCRIPTION: This shallow-water species is one of the few olives to vary little in colour and shape, although shells may be bleached white by being placed in hot ashes. The creamy white background is overlaid with light brown lines and squiggles. The spire is high, and the shell has a slender, fusiform shape.
DISTRIBUTION: Australia; New Guinea

OLIVA OLIVA

AUTHORITY: (Linnaeus 1758)
COMMON NAME: Common olive
GENERAL DESCRIPTION: This species, which is the true type of the genus, exhibits an enormous range in colour and pattern, and this variety has resulted in a large number of names being given to it in the past. However, the characteristic elongated shape with a short spire and the constant dark grey colour of the interior should readily distinguish this from other species. It occurs in sandy areas in shallow water.
  A purely black form occurs, and this was given the name *O. orieola* by Lamarck in 1811.
DISTRIBUTION: Tropical Indo-Pacific

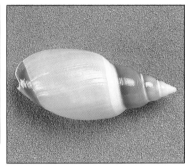

ANCILLA CINGULATA

AUTHORITY: (Sowerby 1830)
COMMON NAME: Honey-banded ancilla
GENERAL DESCRIPTION: This beautiful, thin, fragile shell, with its rounded glossy whorls and high spire, is restricted in distribution to Australian waters, where it is found on sand flats in shallow water. The apex and shoulder of the body whorl are white, which contrasts with the honey or amber colour of the early whorls. The body whorl is a delicate pink. Iredale gave it the name *Ancillista velesiana* in 1936, and it is sometimes described under that synonym.
DISTRIBUTION: East and southeast Australia

MARGIN SHELLS

family Marginellidae

This is a large family of usually small, highly polished shells with over 600 species, the majority of which are found in shallow sandy areas, especially the tropical seas around west Africa. The name derives from the thickened outer lip of the aperture, and the columella has several distinct ridges or plications. The classification of this group is highly complex and is based chiefly on anatomical features.

MITRE SHELLS

family Mitridae

These small to large, smooth or spirally sculptured shells possess tall, pointed spires and narrow, elongated apertures, with plicate columellas. The shells tend to be brightly coloured, but they are often covered by encrusting algae. There is no operculum. The animal is found in sand or mud, under rocks or coral as well as among algal beds, where it feeds on sipunculid worms. The family contains several hundred carnivorous species, which are distributed throughout warm seas worldwide.

PRUNUM LABIATA

AUTHORITY: (Kiener 1841)
COMMON NAME: Royal marginella
GENERAL DESCRIPTION: This solid, medium-sized, shallow-water sand dweller has a flat, heavily callused spire and a slightly inflated posterior. It is a rich cream colour, which contrasts markedly with the thickened yellow lip, which shows evidence of small denticles.
DISTRIBUTION: Lower Caribbean to Brazil

MITRA MITRA

AUTHORITY: (Linnaeus 1758)
COMMON NAME: Episcopal mitre
GENERAL DESCRIPTION: This well-known and attractive shell is probably the largest in the family, and it is a shallow-water sand dweller. The rather heavy, elongate shell is coloured by rich, red squares and blotches on a white background. The tall spire is longer than the body whorl, which has almost straight sides. The aperture is a creamy yellow, the lips are dentate, and the columella bears strong plaits.
DISTRIBUTION: Indo-Pacific

MITRE SHELLS

family Costellariidae

Members of this family closely resemble shells of the Mitridae family, and they were at one time classed with them. They live in a variety of habitats in intertidal to deep water, feeding on gastropods and other small invertebrates.

NUTMEG SHELLS

family Cancellariidae

These small to medium-sized, strongly reticulated shells occur throughout the world, mostly in warm or tropical seas. They have elevated spires and expanded apertures, which often have thickened, crenulated outer lips. The columella is usually strongly ridged, and there is no operculum. Nutmegs are vegetable feeders, living in moderate to deep water on sand or rubble. The animal has a distinctive radula and is believed to feed on small protozoa.

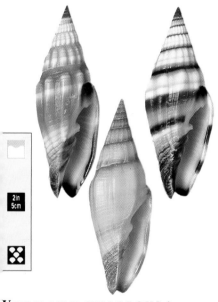

2in
5cm

VEXILLUM VULPECULA

AUTHORITY: (Linnaeus 1758)
COMMON NAME: Little fox mitre
GENERAL DESCRIPTION: This is a well-known, popular and highly variable species, as can be seen from the three specimens illustrated, all of which were collected in the central Philippines. The body whorl is longer than the spire, and the apex is usually broken off. The aperture is long and narrow, and there is a swelling at the top of the aperture. Colours can range from cream to brown, with red, black or orange spiral bands. They inhabit shallow sandy areas.
DISTRIBUTION: Indo-Pacific

1½in
3cm

CANCELLARIA RETICULATA

AUTHORITY: (Linnaeus 1767)
COMMON NAME: Common nutmeg
GENERAL DESCRIPTION: This is perhaps the best known member of the family. Its relatively large, solid shell is decorated by a series of low, spiral cords, which are, in turn, crossed by axial ridges to produce a reticulate pattern. The background colour is cream or off-white, and the bands are dark brown. It occurs subtidally down to about 60ft (20m).
DISTRIBUTION: Southeastern United States to Brazil

SUPER FAMILY
CONOIDEA

CONE SHELLS
family Conidae

The shell is often covered by a periostracum, which may be coarse or smooth. There is an elongate aperture and smooth columella. The operculum is small and elongate; it may even be absent. Cones live from intertidal to deep water, and may be found under rocks and coral or buried in sand. They are carnivorous and highly developed poison glands and the modified, harpoon-like radular teeth are used to capture their prey. It has been reported that some species, notably *Conus geographus*, have caused human deaths. There are over 300 species.

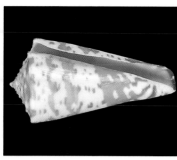

CONUS SCULLETTI

AUTHORITY: Marsh 1962
COMMON NAME: Scullett's cone
GENERAL DESCRIPTION: This species has been only relatively recently described, and the shell illustrated was obtained at a depth of some 480ft (145m) off Cape Moreton, Queensland. It is a slender, fairly light shell, with a low spire. The body whorl may be straight sided or slightly concave. The background colour is off-white or cream, with light brown patterning.
DISTRIBUTION: South Queensland and north New South Wales

CONUS GEOGRAPHUS

AUTHORITY: Linnaeus 1758
COMMON NAME: Geography cone
GENERAL DESCRIPTION: This large but surprisingly light, shallow-water species can eat fish as large as itself, and its poisoned venom is known to have killed at least one human, the shell concerned now being in the British Museum (Natural History). The aperture of this species is especially large, and the body whorl is inflated. The base of the body whorl is encircled by several ridges. The background colour varies from bluish-white to cream, and the markings are various shades of brown. The two shells illustrated originated from the Philippines.
DISTRIBUTION: Indo-Pacific

CONUS TESSULATUS

AUTHORITY: Born 1778
COMMON NAME: Tessellated cone
GENERAL DESCRIPTION: The tesselated (or tesselate) cone, with its low spire, violet-tinged columella base, rounded body whorl and its pattern of red or orange markings on a white background is a pretty sight, which would grace any collection. The early whorls and slightly blunt apex are raised, and spiral ridges usually occur on the whorls. In old specimens, the base of the columella may be white, rather than violet.
DISTRIBUTION: Indo-Pacific

TURRID SHELLS

family Turridae

Although these small to medium-sized shells often resemble other groups in shape, they are readily distinguished by the apertural notch on the shoulder of the body whorl. The siphonal canal is frequently lengthened to produce a spindle-like appearance. A leaf-shaped operculum is small and horny, but may be asent. Turrids, which number over 1,000 named species, inhabit intertidal to very deep water, sheltering under rocks or coral in sand or muddy areas. They are carnivorous, feeding on marine worms and other small invertebrates. Some possess harpoon-like teeth.

ONUS TEXTILE

THORITY: Linnaeus 1758
MMON NAME: Textile cone
NERAL DESCRIPTION: The textile or cloth of gold ne is perhaps one of the best known and more attractive ecies. It is, however, one of the most venomous of the nes and has been responsible for poisoning humans. The ort spire has straight or slightly concave sides, while the dy whorl may have more markedly convex sides. The long erture reveals a glossy white inteior. The shell shows nsiderable variation in form, colour and weight, and several ecies have been created from it. The smaller, blue form is e of these, being known as *Conus euetrios;* this specimen rom Mozambique.
STRIBUTION: Indo-Pacific

GEMMULA KIENERI

AUTHORITY: (Doumet 1840)
COMMON NAME: Kiener's turrid
GENERAL DESCRIPTION: This beautiful species, with its sculpture of brown spiral beads and the extended siphonal canal, would grace any collection. The spire is tall, and the body whorl is inflated at the centre, before tapering to the canal. The off-white or cream background is patterned in brown and reddish-brown, and there are fine brown dashes on the lower part of the body whorl. It has a wide distribution, and examples have been obtained from Japan, the China Sea and the Philippines, although the specimen shown here comes from Cape Moreton, Queensland.
DISTRIBUTION: West Pacific; Australia

AUGER SHELLS
family Terebridae

These small to large, elongate shells have a sharply pointed spire and a small aperture with a thin outer lip. The shell lacks a periostracum, but the surface may be sculptured or smooth and is often brightly coloured. The animal, which has a small, horny operculum, lives in sand or sandy muds in both intertidal and subtidal warm and temperate waters, where it feeds on marine worms. The family contains about 300 species.

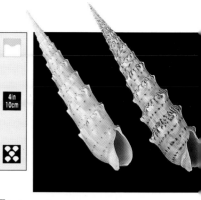

TEREBRA CRENULATA

AUTHORITY: (Linnaeus 1758)
COMMON NAME: Crenulated auger
GENERAL DESCRIPTION: The crenulated or notched auger has a rather stocky shell. It is a medium-sized species, with variable sculpturing and colour pattern, as shown by the two examples illustrated here. The darker of the two shells comes from the Solomon Islands, while the lighter specimen is from Tahiti. Some specimens have almost smooth, straight-sided whorls; others have prominent nodules below the suture. The species occurs in sandy areas in shallow water.
DISTRIBUTION: Indo-Pacific

TEREBRA MACULATA

AUTHORITY: (Linnaeus 1758)
COMMON NAME: Marlinspike auger
GENERAL DESCRIPTION: The shell is extremely thick and heavy, and it is the largest species in the family, the present world record size being over 10in (25cm) in length. The shell has a very tall spire, and there are about 15 slightly convex-sided whorls. The body whorl is narrow and rounded, with an elongate aperture. The background colour is cream or light fawn, and the spiral patterning is brown or greyish-blue. It occurs in shallow water in sand.
DISTRIBUTION: Indo-Pacific

TEREBRA SUBULATA

AUTHORITY: (Linnaeus 1767)
COMMON NAME: Subulate auger
GENERAL DESCRIPTION: This strikingly coloured shell is probably one of the best known of the family. It has over 20 sharply elongated, slightly convex-sided whorls. The body whorl, as in all augers, narrows to form a short canal. The background of cream or beige is patterned with two distinct spiral rows of squarish, dark brown blotches. The species is also known as the chocolate spotted auger because of its bright coloration. It occurs in sandy areas in shallow water.
DISTRIBUTION: Indo-Pacific

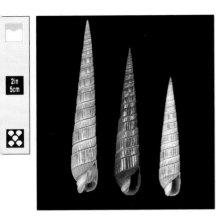

DUPLICARIA DUPLICATA

AUTHORITY: (Linnaeus 1758)
COMMON NAME: Duplicate auger
GENERAL DESCRIPTION: This medium-sized, highly glossy shell is sculptured by a spiral groove on each whorl, crossed by numerous grooves running parallel to the axis. It is highly variable in colour, as can be seen from the three shells illustrated. It occurs in sandy areas in shallow water.
DISTRIBUTION: Indian Ocean; west Pacific

ARCHITECTONICA PERDIX

AUTHORITY: (Hinds 1844)
COMMON NAME: Partridge sundial
GENERAL DESCRIPTION: This small, sand-dwelling shell has the characteristic spiral and beaded umbilicus, which create the staircase effect. The colour varies from off-white to cream with darker brown spiral bands and blotches, the sculpture consisting of weak, closely spaced striae. The shell illustrated comes from Keppel Bay, Queensland. It is unusual to find specimens with undamaged apertures.
DISTRIBUTION: West Pacific; Indian Ocean

SUPER FAMILY

ARCHITECTONICOIDEA

SUNDIAL SHELLS

family Architectonicidae

This is a small family of flat, disc-like shells in which the relatively large and open umbilicus produces a staircase appearance, which results in these shells being known as staircase shells. The animal has a horny operculum, which normally has a tooth-like process on its inner surface. They generally occur in water water, where they live in sandy areas and feed on corals and sea anemones.

PHILIPPIA RADIATA

AUTHORITY: (Röding 1798)
COMMON NAME: Radial sundial
GENERAL DESCRIPTION: This small species has a rather humped spire and a small, open umbilicus, with the base tending to be convex. The shell's surface is smooth and moderately glossy. It is cream in colour with a distinct spiral orange band and axial streaks. It was described by Iredale in 1931 under the name *Philippia stipator*. It occurs in sandy areas in shallow water.
DISTRIBUTION: West Pacific; Indian Ocean

SUPER FAMILY
PHILINOIDEA

This superfamily contains a group of molluscs that are generally devoid of shells. It includes the nudibranchs or sea slugs and sea hares. A few members of this super-family do, however, possess shells that are of interest to the collector, and these are known generally as bubble shells.

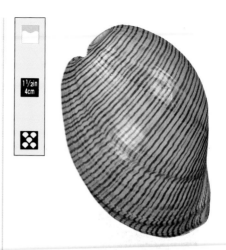

1½in
4cm

BUBBLE SHELLS
family Hydatinidae

The shells within this family are small to medium and thin. They have a depressed spire and, often, coloured banding. The animal, which does not have an operculum, may be found in sandy pools or beneath rocks in the intertidal zone. They are mostly carnivores, feeding chiefly on marine worms, although some feed on algae.

HYDATINA PHYSIS

AUTHORITY: (Linnaeus 1758)
COMMON NAME: Paper bubble shell
GENERAL DESCRIPTION: This is probably the best known of the bubble shells. It is a thin, rather fragile shell, with a depressed spire and an enlarged, bulbous body whorl. The flared aperture reveals a white interior, while the exterior is cream or yellowish, with pretty olive green to dark brown banding. It occurs in sandy mud, on banked-up weed growths such as eel-grass or even on coral reefs.
DISTRIBUTION: Indo-Pacific

BUBBLE SHELLS
family Bullidae
Medium-sized shells with an inflated body
whorl and sunken spire. The aperture is
expanded and differs from the Hydatinids
by the presence of a callus deposit on the
columella. Bullids occur in sand or on coral
in intertidal and shallow water. The animal
feeds on green algae.

BUBBLE SHELLS
family Hamineidae
These small, thin shells are usually white or
yellow. They may be smooth or be covered
with fine spiral grooves. The animals, which
live in sand or sandy mud from intertidal to
deep water, are all herbivores.

1¼in
3cm

1½in
4cm

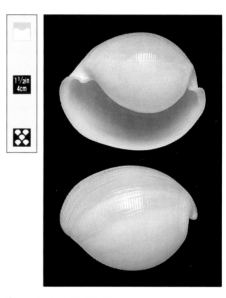

ATYS NAUCUM
AUTHORITY: (Linnaeus 1758)
COMMON NAME: White Pacific atys
GENERAL DESCRIPTION: This fine, lightweight shell is
white in colour and is decorated with a series of fine spiral
striations. It is globose – living up to the name bubble shell –
and the posterior lip extends upwards, almost over the
depressed, virtually absent spire. As can be seen in the
photograph, the columella has a small fold or plication. The
shell illustrated comes from the central Philippines, and the
species can be found on sand or sandy mud from the
intertidal zone down to deep water throughout the Indo-Pacific
area.
DISTRIBUTION: Indo-Pacific

ULLA STRIATA
THORITY: Bruguière 1792
MMON NAME: Common Atlantic bubble
NERAL DESCRIPTION: This pretty but sturdy shell
,sually ovate, and the spire is depressed. The body whorl is
npressed at the anterior. The shells are extremely variable
attern, having brown, white or grey blotches. The aperture
vhite. The two examples illustrated, which indicate the
ge of colours, were collected off Yucatan, Mexico.
STRIBUTION: Florida to Brazil; Mediterranean

CLASS
BIVALVIA

The shells of bivalves are composed of two pieces – valves – which are joined together by an elastic ligament. Most bivalves have a large, muscular foot, a pair of large mantle lobes responsible for secreting the shell-making material, and inhalent and exhalent siphons. They are found in the sea and in freshwater worldwide.

SUPER FAMILY

LIMOPSOIDEA

BITTERSWEET CLAMS
family Glycimerididae

Bittersweet clams have thick, rounded, heavy and porcellaneous shells, covered by a thick skin or periostracum. The hinge plate bears many fine, radiating, interlocking hinge teeth. There are more than 100 species (some authorities say as many as 150), which are distributed mainly in the Indo-Pacific in sandy, shallow waters. Many are used for food.

4in
10cm

GLYCYMERUS GIGANTEA

AUTHORITY: (Reeve 1843)
COMMON NAME: Giant bittersweet
GENERAL DESCRIPTION: This species grows to 4in (10cm) and is locally common offshore in the Gulf of California at depths of 20–40ft (7–12m). The attractive shells are often washed ashore following storms. The symmetrical valves are thick and very heavy. The white interior shows brown or purple staining, while the off-white or cream exterior is decorated with reddish-brown zigzag marks
DISTRIBUTION: Gulf of California

SUPER FAMILY
MYTILOIDEA

MUSSEL SHELLS
family Mytilidae

The Mytilidae or true mussels are found throughout the world in shallow intertidal waters. The shells are relatively thin but strong, elongated and are covered by a thick periostracum. The interior is often pearly and has weakly developed hinge teeth. Most species live in colonies attached to rocks, stones and so forth by a byssus (group of filaments). Some species, however, burrow into rock or coral.

4¹/₂in
11.5cm

PERNA CANALICULUS

AUTHORITY: (Gmelin 1791)
COMMON NAME: Channel mussel
GENERAL DESCRIPTION: This is a large, attractive species, with a green periostracum and radial rows of black lines. The umbones are rounded, although somewhat pointed, and there is a rudimentary tooth structure. A long ligament joins the valves. It can grow to 6in (15cm), although smaller specimens are more common, and it is found on rocks exposed at low tide around the coasts of New Zealand. The shell illustrated comes from the Hauraki Gulf region of North Island; many are exported to the UK for food.
DISTRIBUTION: New Zealand

6in
5cm

MYTILUS EDULIS

AUTHORITY: (Linnaeus 1758)
COMMON NAME: Common blue mussel
GENERAL DESCRIPTION: The common blue or edible mussel has been well known to man as a source of food since pre-historic times, being plentiful on rocky shorelines throughout the world. The triangular blue shell with its pearly interior is generally found on rocky shores from the intertidal area down to 30ft (10m). The valves are joined by a long, thin ligament. In recent years it has provided a new industry, being farmed in many areas in beds or offshore on raftings.
DISTRIBUTION: Worldwide

SUPER FAMILY
PTERIOIDEA

WING AND PEARL OYSTERS
family Pteriidae

The Pteriidae family includes the wing oysters, which are characterized by well-developed, wing-like extensions of the hinge-line and by a byssus, by which they attach themselves to coral rubble, rocks and sea fans. The family also contains pearl oysters, which are rounder. Their highly developed pearly interior is used to produce articles for the curio trade, and many species are used in the production of pearls, both natural and cultured. They mainly occur in tropical seas.

8in
20cm

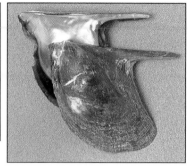

PTERIA PENGUIN

AUTHORITY: (Röding 1798)
COMMON NAME: Penguin wing oyster
GENERAL DESCRIPTION: The penguin wing oyster has a fragile, ovate shell with asymmetric valves, the right, or upper, valve being inflated. The interior is pearly. It inhabits shallow waters and normally grows to 6in (15cm) but sometimes reaches 10in (25cm). The illustrated example, which is from the central Philippines, clearly exhibits the characteristic extension of the hinge-line from which the common name derives.
DISTRIBUTION: Indo-Pacific

HAMMER OYSTERS

family Malleidae

The hammer oysters comprise a small group. They have a semi-nacreous interior, while the hinge-line combines with an elongation of the shell body to give a hammer-like appearance. The ligament is accommodated in a small depression in the centre of the top edge of the hinge. Most species live in tropical seas among flattened coral reefs or in rock crevices.

7in
18cm

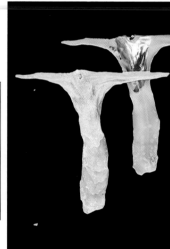

MALLEUS ALBUS

AUTHORITY: (Lamarck 1819)
COMMON NAME: White hammer oyster
GENERAL DESCRIPTION: The white hammer oyster occurs in shallow sandy areas on grass and rock flats throughout the Indo-Pacific, including Australia. The extended hinge-line and elongate body shape of the beige-coloured shell gave rise to its common name. It was greatly sought after by collectors at the beginning of the 19th century, and is still popular with collectors who specialize in bivalves.
DISTRIBUTION: Indo-Pacific

PEN SHELLS

family Pinnidae

The members of this small family of large, thin, fan-shaped shells, are attached to the substrate by means of a fine, silky byssus. In the past this was used as a form of natural silk and formed the basis of a small industry in the area around Taranto in southern Italy. The small amount of byssal silk produced by each mussel together with the introduction of artificial silk have long since made this industry obsolete.

TRUE OYSTERS

family Ostreidae

Members of the oyster family have been used as a source of food since pre-historic times, and they are now cultivated in oyster beds all over the world. The shells are normally irregular in outline and are cemented to rocks or to each other by the lower, left valve.

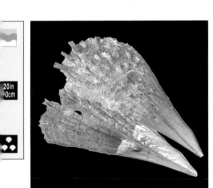

INNA RUDIS

UTHORITY: Linnaeus 1758
OMMON NAME: Rude pen shell
ENERAL DESCRIPTION: The fan-shaped exterior of the de (or rough) pen shell is decorated by a series of low dial ridges, from which arise a series of upturned, hollow ines. The thin, translucent shell is orange-brown or olive own. The interior is smooth but uneven, and there is a arly layer towards the narrower end. It occurs locally shore in sandy areas.
STRIBUTION: Mediterranean to north and west Africa

OSTREA EDULIS

AUTHORITY: Linnaeus 1758
COMMON NAME: Common European oyster
GENERAL DESCRIPTION: This is the edible oyster of culinary fame, which has been farmed commercially in the UK and elsewhere for centuries. It is roughly circular in outline, with a virtually flat lower valve and a slightly inflated upper valve. It has a greyish-white interior, unlike the introduced Portuguese oyster *Crassostera angulara*, which tends to be irregularly elongate and have a white interior. The example illustrated is from Langstone Bridge, Hampshire, UK.
DISTRIBUTION: Western Europe; Mediterranean

SUPER FAMILY

PECTINOIDEA

SCALLOP SHELLS

family Pectinidae

Pectens or scallops are among the best known of the bivalves, and they are extremely popular with collectors because of their attractive colours, rounded outline and varied surface sculpture. There are several hundred species, distributed throughout the world, occurring in both deep and shallow habitats. The right valve has an anterior byssal notch, and the hinge-line is produced to form two "ears", one on each side of the umbones. Many scallops swim by rapidly opening and closing their valves. Several species are fished commercially as food.

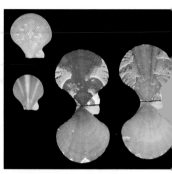

CHLAMYS TIGERINA

AUTHORITY: (Muller 1776)

COMMON NAME: Tiger scallop

GENERAL DESCRIPTION: This small, rounded shell, which tapers sharply at the umbones, has unequal ears. The symmetrical valves have a smooth but dull surface. It is relatively common in deeper waters around northern Europe but tends to be scarce in collections since it is not thought commercially viable by North Sea fishermen. The shells illustrated, which exhibit some of the diverse colour forms, were dredged at about 500ft (150m) off southern Iceland.

DISTRIBUTION: West Europe; Iceland; Norway to Spain

ARGOPECTEN CIRCULARIS

AUTHORITY: (Sowerby 1835)

COMMON NAME: Circular scallop

GENERAL DESCRIPTION: The circular scallop has, as the name suggests, a rounded shell with inflated, equal valves and ears. The valves are traversed by about 18 raised, rounded ribs. The shells show considerable variation in colour and pattern, as may be seen from those illustrated. The circular scallop lives in subtidal waters, down to depths of over 300ft (100m), and is fished commercially for food.

DISTRIBUTION: Western Mexico to Peru

MESOPEPLUM TASMANICUM

AUTHORITY: (Adams and Angus 1863)

COMMON NAME: Tasman scallop

GENERAL DESCRIPTION: The Tasman scallop has rounded equal valves, but unequal ears. The upper valve is normally pink to reddish-purple, while the lower valve is white or pink. Both valves are traversed by five strong radial ridges, with numerous smaller, finer ones between them. It is relatively uncommon, occurring at depths of 60–250ft (18–75m). The shell seen here came from Port Lincoln.

DISTRIBUTION: Tasmania; South Australia

LYROPECTEN NODOSA

AUTHORITY: (Linnaeus 1758)
COMMON NAME: Lion's paw
GENERAL DESCRIPTION: This shell, with its fan-shaped, equal valves, is greatly sought after by collectors. Each valve has seven or eight rounded radial ribs, which normally bear large rounded nodules. The ears are not equal, the anterior being slightly larger. The colour is generally brown or red but occasionally very desirable yellow or orange forms also occur. The interior is purplish-brown. It is found offshore down to about 100ft (30m).
DISTRIBUTION: Southeast United States to Brazil

PATINOPECTEN CAURINUS

AUTHORITY: (Gould 1850)
COMMON NAME: Giant Pacific scallop
GENERAL DESCRIPTION: The Pacific scallop is possibly the largest of the scallop species, achieving up to 7in (18cm) across. It has rounded, equal and slightly convex valves, with strongly developed, low and rounded, radial ribs. The upper, left valve is beige or pale brown in colour, while the lower, right valve tends to be pale cream. The anterior ear is slightly larger than the posterior ear. This species has proved to be ideal for commercial fishing.
DISTRIBUTION: Alaska to California

THORNY OYSTERS
family Spondylidae

These close relations to scallops live permanently attached to corals or rocks. The marine growths on their elongated spines act as camouflage for the oyster. They vary greatly in shape, size and colour, but all have a characteristic ball-and-socket hinge structure which is not dissimilar to the human elbow. Their attractive shapes, long spines and varied colours make perfect examples of this group highly prized.

3in
7.5cm

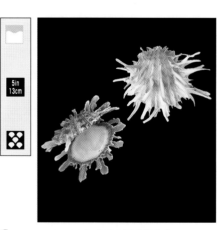

5in
13cm

SPONDYLUS PRINCEPS

AUTHORITY: Broderip 1833
COMMON NAME: Pacific thorny oyster
GENERAL DESCRIPTION: The heavy shell of this extremely variable species bears long, thick but blunt spines. Both valves are inflated and equal, and the ears are small. The valves are usually red or pink, while the spines are generally white, which combine to give a highly attractive appearance. Perfect examples are greatly sought after. They occur offshore attached to coral or rocks.
DISTRIBUTION: Gulf of California to Panama

SPONDYLUS WRIGHTIANUS

AUTHORITY: Crosse 1872
COMMON NAME: Wright's thorny oyster
GENERAL DESCRIPTION: Wright's thorny oyster is perhaps one of the most outstanding species in this remarkable group. Its long spines are often twice the overall size of the shell, and they are interspersed by several finer spines. The small, rounded valves are not equal, the lower one being flat, while the upper valve is inflated. The colour varies from off-white to pink or lavender, and the largest spines often remain white. It is native to west Australia, where it occurs offshore down to about 150ft (50m).
DISTRIBUTION: West Australia

SUPER FAMILY

TRIGONIIDEA

BROOCH CLAMS

family Trigonidae

Often referred to as living fossils, the few Australian species of brooch clam are all that remain of a group that was dominant in Jurassic seas some 200 million years ago. The triangular shells have three hinge teeth in one valve and two in the other. The interior is pearly and highly iridescent, the shells often being collected and used to make jewellery.

SUPER FAMILY

LUCINOIDEA

LUCINA CLAMS

family Lucinidae

The lucina clams are a large family. The shells are thick, white and circular to oval, with a very small lunule and a long ligament, which may be external or internal. The anterior muscle scar is relatively narrow and elongate and, unlike the similar Venus shells, there is no pallial sinus. They inhabit both shallow and deep water worldwide but prefer warmer waters, where they burrow into mud or sand.

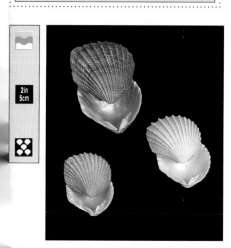

2in
5cm

4in
10cm

NEOTRIGONIA BEDNALLI

AUTHORITY: Verco 1907

COMMON NAME: Bednall's brooch clam

GENERAL DESCRIPTION: This small, rather solid, triangular shell may be readily recognized. It has a rich lavender or pale orange iridescent interior, and the exterior bears strongly granulate radial ribbing. There is a complex, V-shaped hinge. It is common around southeast Australia on mud in offshore waters down to about 150ft (50m).

DISTRIBUTION: Southeast Australia

CODAKIA TIGERINA

AUTHORITY: (Linnaeus 1758)

COMMON NAME: Pacific tiger lucina

GENERAL DESCRIPTION: This attractive shell has a distinctive, reticulated, chalky white exterior, which contrasts with the interior of pale yellow bordered by pinkish-red. The hinge area and ligament are large; the teeth are small. The species occurs throughout the Indo-Pacific from extreme low water to depths of over 60ft (20m).

DISTRIBUTION: Indo-Pacific

CARDITA CLAMS
family Carditidae

The distinctive cardita clams, with their strongly ribbed, boat-shaped shells, anteriorly placed beaks, external ligament and crenulate internal margins, have a worldwide distribution. There is no pallial sinus, and some species have a byssus. Most species in this group retain their young inside the mantle cavity.

CARDITA CRASSICOSTA

AUTHORITY: (Lamarck 1819)
COMMON NAME: Leafy cardita
GENERAL DESCRIPTION: The leafy cardita, which is also known as the Australian cardita, has a distinctive shell with four or five large radial ribs, which are normally covered by strongly fluted scales. It is common from low-tide level down to depths of over 300ft (90m). There is considerable variation in colour, as can be seen in the shells shown here, which came from the Sulu Sea, between the Philippines and Borneo.

DISTRIBUTION: West and south Australia; Philippines

CARDITA LATICOSTATA

AUTHORITY: Sowerby 1833
COMMON NAME: Wide-ribbed cardita
GENERAL DESCRIPTION: This thick and solid shell has about 15 ribs, which radiate from the umbones and which often bear small scales. There is a strong hinge and two large cardinal teeth. It is normally off-white with bands or flecks of various shades of brown. The interior is white. It is common and can be found intertidally down to about 170ft (55m).

DISTRIBUTION: Gulf of California to north Peru

SUPER FAMILY

CHAMOIDEA

JEWEL BOXES

family Chamidae

These attractive, thick and heavy shelled bivalves bear a strong resemblance to the thorny oysters, but they may easily be distinguished by their rudimentary hinge structure. Most species within the family are cemented to rocks, to coral or to each other. They possess foliated spines and scales and live in shallow tropical waters.

SUPER FAMILY

CARDIOIDEA

COCKLE SHELLS

family Cardiidae

This large, well-known family has a worldwide distribution and includes numerous edible species. The shells vary in size from small to very large, and most exhibit a radial sculpture of ribbing. They have a rounded, oval outline and large, inflated, centrally placed umbones. There are two equal adductor scars and no pallial sinus. The animal has a large foot and is capable of leaping several inches through the water when disturbed. There are over 200 species in the family.

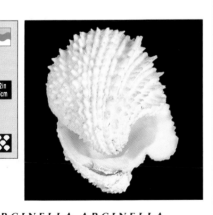

ACANTHOCARDIA ECHINATA

AUTHORITY: (Linnaeus 1758)
COMMON NAME: European prickly cockle
GENERAL DESCRIPTION: The inflated round or oval shell has 18–22 radiating ribs bearing a central row of sharp spines. The broad umbones rise above the hinge-line of the equal valves. It is of a pale yellow or brown colour, occasionally mottled, and the inner edge of the valves is crenulate. It lives in sandy areas from just offshore to considerable depths.
DISTRIBUTION: West Europe; northwest Africa; Mediterranean

ARCINELLA ARCINELLA

AUTHORITY: (Linnaeus 1767)
COMMON NAME: True spiny jewel box
GENERAL DESCRIPTION: The triangular shell is solid and strong. It is normally white and has between 16 and 35 radial ribs, bearing both long and short spines. The interior may be stained pink, yellow or purple. It is normally cemented to a firm surface but may occasionally be free. It occurs from low water to depths of over 250ft (75m).
DISTRIBUTION: West Indies to Brazil

PLAGIOCARDIUM SETOSUM

AUTHORITY: (Redfield 1846)
COMMON NAME: Hairy cockle
GENERAL DESCRIPTION: The hairy cockle has a typical oval cockle shape with numerous ribs radiating from the umbonal area. These ribs bear small, blunt nodules. The large, inflated valves are equal. The shells are beige or light brown and normally patterned by intermittent darker bands. The interior is white, and the shell margins are crenulate.
DISTRIBUTION: Southwest Pacific; north Australia

SUPER FAMILY
TRIDACNOIDEA

GIANT CLAMS
family Tridacnidae

The members of this group have thick, heavy shells with strong radial ribs, which normally bear scales. The shell edges are strongly scalloped and interlock. They possess a byssus and lie with their hinge area on the sea-floor so that the gaping valves face upwards towards the surface to allow sunlight to reach the symbiotic algae in the large, fleshy mantle lobes with which the animal feeds. There are about a dozen species inhabiting tropical Indo-Pacific waters.

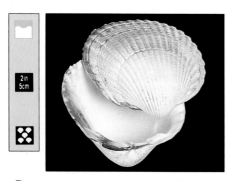

CERASTODERMA EDULE

AUTHORITY: (Linnaeus 1758)
COMMON NAME: Common European cockle
GENERAL DESCRIPTION: This well-known species is widely used for food and is often farmed commercially. The medium-sized, oval shell has 22–28 radial ribs, each of which bears scale-like spines. The colour varies from dirty white through pale yellow to various shades of brown. The interior is white, and the posterior muscle scar is frequently stained brown. It is widely distributed and often abundant in intertidal sands and mud flats.
DISTRIBUTION: Norway to northwest Africa

HIPPOPUS HIPPOPUS

AUTHORITY: (Linnaeus 1758)
COMMON NAME: Bear's claw clam
GENERAL DESCRIPTION: The triangular shape, white interior and strongly fluted off-white exterior mottled with orange, yellow or crimson made the bear's claw clam popular with Victorians for its decorative potential. This popularity has continued to the present day and has resulted in so much over-fishing that trade in this species is now prohibited. It is, indeed, a striking shell, with its deep, inflated valves. These are strongly sculptured and bear about seven large and numerous small ribs. The long hinge-line runs about half the length of the shell. It occurs on coral reefs in shallow water.
DISTRIBUTION: Southwest Pacific

SUPER FAMILY

MACTROIDEA

MACTRA CLAMS

family Mactridae

Members of this family, sometimes called trough shells, have a worldwide distribution in shallow waters, and there are about 100 species. They have no byssus, and the shells may be smooth or possess concentric sculpturing. The triangular shape, centrally placed umbones, deep pallial sinus and two equal muscle scars plus internal ligament readily distinguish this group. The animal burrows in sand, and many species are edible.

SUPER FAMILY

SOLENOIDEA

RAZOR SHELLS

family Solenidae

Solens or razor shells are thin and elongate, and they have parallel dorsal and ventral margins, which make them ideally suited for burrowing into sand or mud. The ligament is external. The hinge has a single cardinal tooth in each valve. There are no lateral teeth. They occur throughout the world, and many species are fished commercially.

MACTRA CORALLINA

AUTHORITY: (Linnaeus 1758)
COMMON NAME: Rayed mactra
GENERAL DESCRIPTION: This smooth, glossy and light triangular shell is a pale reddish-brown, and a series of lighter cream-coloured, broad and narrow radial rays is often present. The interior is a pale violet. The ligament is external. It lives in clean sand in shallow water, and specimens are often cast ashore after storms. The shell illustrated is from Camber Sands, on the south coast of England.
DISTRIBUTION: UK to the Mediterranean

SOLENS MARGINATUS

AUTHORITY: Montagu 1803
COMMON NAME: European razor clam
GENERAL DESCRIPTION: The long, straight-sided valves, with their truncated ends and single cardinal tooth, may be readily distinguished from the jackknife clams. The shells are beige or a dirty-looking yellow, with a mid-brown periostracum. The species is characterized by a groove that runs just behind and parallel to the anterior margin.
DISTRIBUTION: West Europe, Mediterranean; west Africa

SUPER FAMILY
SOLENOIDEA

JACKKNIFE CLAMS
family Cultellidae

Known as jackknife clams, these appear remarkably similar to the true razor shells, but they may be readily distinguished by the cardinal and lateral teeth – razor shells have no laterals. Most species have the elongate razor shape, but some are squarer and boat-shaped. They inhabit shallow sandy areas and have a worldwide distribution.

SUPER FAMILY
TELLINOIDEA

TELLINS
family Tellinidae

Tellins have small to medium-sized shells, which tend to be flattened, thin and rounded in front and angular behind. The ligament is external and the hinge has two small cardinal teeth in each valve. There is a well-defined pallial sinus. They are also known as butterfly shells, and there are over 200 species worldwide, occurring in shallow water where they burrow into sand or mud.

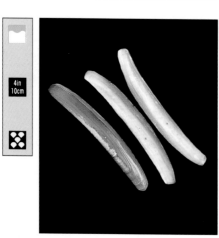

4in
10cm

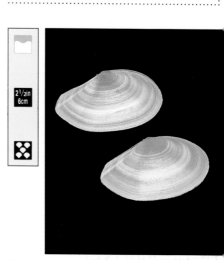

2¹/₂in
6cm

ENSIS ENSIS

AUTHORITY: (Linnaeus 1758)
COMMON NAME: Narrow jackknife clam
GENERAL DESCRIPTION: The fragile, elongated, slightly curved shell, with its external ligament, is covered by a pale olive green periostracum, which is ornamented by concentric growth lines. The right valve has one small cardinal tooth and one lateral tooth; the left valve has two cardinal and two lateral teeth. It occurs from low-water mark down to 250ft (75m).
DISTRIBUTION: Norway to Mediterranean

TELLINA ALBINELLA

AUTHORITY: Lamarck 1819
COMMON NAME: Little white tellin
GENERAL DESCRIPTION: The little white tellin is something of a misnomer since, although white shells do occur, it is more commonly pink or pale orange with delicate white concentric lines. The thin, shiny shell is sculptured by a series of fine, crowded concentric striations. The posterior beak-like part of the shell tends to be compressed.
DISTRIBUTION: South coasts of Australia

HEART CLAMS

family Glossidae

Although few species exist today in cool and tropical seas, the family is well represented in fossil records. The thick, inflated shells have prominent beaks or umbones which are turned in on themselves producing a distinctive ram's horn effect. The ligament is external, and the shell surface may be smooth or ribbed.

VENUS CLAMS

family Veneridae

The Veneridae family contains over 400 species, which are distributed worldwide. The solid-walled shells exhibit a variety of shapes, textures and colours, but all possess a pallial sinus. Most inhabit shallow water, although some prefer ocean depths. Many species are used for food.

3¹/₂in
9cm

2¹/₂in
6cm

GLOSSUS HUMANUS

AUTHORITY: Linnaeus 1758
COMMON NAME: Ox-heart clam
GENERAL DESCRIPTION: The common name for this species is derived from its characteristic shape, the shell being covered by a fine, glossy brown skin or periostracum. The hinge bears three cardinal teeth in each valve, and there is no pallial sinus. The shell is yellow-brown in colour and bears numerous growth lines. It lives in sand or mud at depths ranging from 26 to 1,000ft (8–300m).
DISTRIBUTION: Norway to Mediterranean

VENUS VERRUCOSA

AUTHORITY: (Linnaeus 1758)
COMMON NAME: Warty Venus
GENERAL DESCRIPTION: This solid and heavy medium-sized species has equal, rather inflated valves, which are sculptured with strong, concentric ridges. These tend to become nodular towards the anterior and posterior edges. The warty Venus, which is an edible species, occurs from extreme low-tide zone down to 40ft (12m); the shell illustrated is from shallow water off Cadiz, Spain.
DISTRIBUTION: Northeast Atlantic to the Mediterranean

LIOCONCHA CASTRENSIS

AUTHORITY: (Linnaeus 1758)
COMMON NAME: Chocolate-flamed Venus
GENERAL DESCRIPTION: The chocolate-flamed or Camp Pitar Venus is widely distributed throughout the Indo-Pacific, including Australia, and it is common in shallow sandy bays. The cream surface of the round or oval shells is overlain by vivid dark brown zigzag lines, which vary considerably, and no two shells appear identical. The rounded umbones are prominent. There is a large escutcheon, an internal ligament and a shallow pallial sinus. The three shells illustrated are from the central Philippines.
DISTRIBUTION: Indo-Pacific

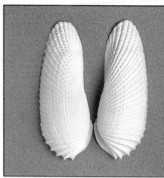

CYRTOPLEURA COSTATA

AUTHORITY: (Linnaeus 1758)
COMMON NAME: Angel wing
GENERAL DESCRIPTION: The angel wing occurs from the southeast United States to Brazil and may burrow as deep as 3ft (1m) into the mud substrate. It has a beautiful thin, elongated, delicate white shell. The radially ridged valves resemble a pair of wings when they are opened out on the sand. The species can grow to 7½in (20cm), although recently caught specimens rarely exceed 6in (15cm).
DISTRIBUTION: East United States to Brazil

SUPER FAMILY
PHOLADOIDEA

PIDDOCKS AND ANGEL WINGS

family Pholadidae

This family, which contains the piddocks and angel wings, has a worldwide distribution. The thin but strong elongated shells gape at both ends, the ribbed valves possessing accessory plates as well as shelly projections (apophyses) beneath the umbones. They burrow or bore into rock, clay, soft limestones, coral and wood.

PHOLAS DACTYLUS

AUTHORITY: Linnaeus 1758
COMMON NAME: European piddock
GENERAL DESCRIPTION: This species has a thin, britt off-white shell, the valves being sculpted by a series of about 20 circular ridges crossed by about 40 ribs, which radiate from the umbones. It bores into muds, shales, chalk and sandstones and is widely distributed throughout the northea Atlantic and the Mediterranean. The animal has the remarkable property of producing phosphorescent substances, which cause it to glow in the dark with a greenish-blue light.
DISTRIBUTION: Northeast Atlantic; Mediterranean

CLASS
POLYPLACOPHORA

ORDER: NEOLORICATA

Chitons or coat-of-mail shells are worldwide in distribution, and there are over 1,000 living species. The ovate shells are composed of eight plates set into a tough muscular girdle, which enables them to curl up like woodlice. They are mainly vegetarians, but may feed on small invertebrates, and are usually found in shallow water under stones or on rocks.

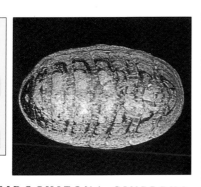

1in
.5cm

EPIDOCHITONA CINEREUS

AUTHORITY: (Linnaeus 1767)
COMMON NAME: Grey chiton
GENERAL DESCRIPTION: This species, which occurs from just below high-tide level down into the subtidal zone, is small and lightweight. The underside of its shell plates is a pale bluish-green. The upper surface is beige to greyish-brown but is normally heavily encrusted. The example illustrated was obtained from the underside of chalk boulders just below high-tide level at Eastbourne, Sussex, UK.
DISTRIBUTION: Scandinavia; west Europe; west Mediterranean

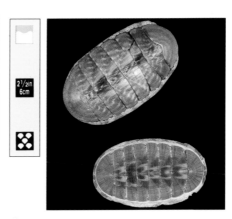

2¹/₂in
6cm

CHITON MAMORATUS

AUTHORITY: Gmelin 1791
COMMON NAME: Marbled chiton
GENERAL DESCRIPTION: This species is relatively common in inter-tidal areas on most rocky shores throughout its range. The smooth upper surface is beige to greyish brown with paler blotches or streaks whilst the girdle has alternating bands of grey or green.
DISTRIBUTION: South-east Florida to West Indies

CLASS
CEPHALOPODA

Cephalopods are a highly evolved group of marine molluscs, which possess a well-developed head with eyes and a ring of 8–10 sucker-bearing arms or tentacles. The mouth has a horny, beak-like structure, which, since all living species are carnivores, is used for tearing their prey. Some species have an external shell, but in most species the shell is reduced and internal or entirely absent. The class includes octopuses and squids as well as the pearly nautilus and paper nautilus.

CHAMBERED NAUTILUS SHELLS
family Nautilidae

The four or five living species of chambered nautilus are the last remnants of a group that dates from the beginning of fossil records. The external shell is divided into chambers, and the animal, which has about 90 tentacles, lives in the last or "body" chamber. The other, earlier chambers are filled with gas, which provides a buoyancy mechanism that permits the nautilus to rise or fall in the ocean depths. The flame-like radial markings on the outer shell surface camouflage the shell by breaking up its outline when it is viewed from below.

NAUTILUS POMPILUS

AUTHORITY: Linnaeus 1758
COMMON NAME: Common chambered nautilus
GENERAL DESCRIPTION: The common nautilus differs from other living species because it has no umbilicus, the body whorl completely covering the earlier whorls. The white or creamy shell is thin and light. It lives in colonies around the Philippines and Palau Islands in the Pacific Ocean, but dead shells are often washed ashore throughout the west Pacific, including Australia. The pearly shell is often used to produce souvenirs such as the half-section illustrated, which shows the internal shell chambers.
DISTRIBUTION: Southwest Pacific

SPIRULAS
family Spirulidae
Squid-like cephalopods, possessing an
internal, loosely coiled, chambered shell,
which is completely embedded within the
living animal. There is only one species.

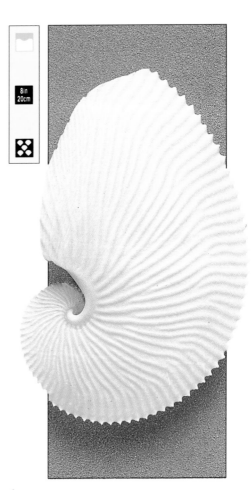

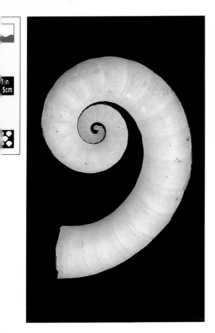

PIRULA SPIRULA

HORITY: (Linnaeus 1758)
MMON NAME: Common spirula
IERAL DESCRIPTION: Shells of this species are
1 washed onto beaches after storms. They may be readily
gnized by the loosely coiled and chambered shell, which,
e, is embedded within the tissues of this deep-water
d. The thin, fragile shell chambers are filled with gas,
:h presumably acts as a means of providing buoyancy.
en the animal dies and its body rots away, the shell floats
e surface. The species lives at depths of 3,000ft
00m) or more.
TRIBUTION: Worldwide

ARGONAUTA ARGO

AUTHORITY: Linnaeus 1758
COMMON NAME: Common paper nautilus
GENERAL DESCRIPTION: The argonaut or paper
nautilus is a free-swimming, octopus-like animal, which
inhabits warm, open seas throughout the world. The beautiful
shell-like structures are not true shells. They are secreted by
two specialized arms of the female for use as a receptacle for
the animal's eggs. Once the eggs hatch the female dies,
releasing the "shell". Numerous low, wavy ridges extend from
the tightly coiled spire to the margin. The structure is off-white
to cream, the early part of the keel and spines being faintly
grey. The male has no shell. The common paper nautilus is
often washed ashore after storms.
DISTRIBUTION: Worldwide

CLASS
SCAPHOPODA

TUSK SHELLS
FAMILY: DENTALIIDAE

Over 1,000 species of tusk shell occur throughout the world in a variety of habitats. They live in sand or mud from shallow water to considerable depths. The shell consists of a simple tube which is open at both ends. They have little use to man, although one North American species was once used for currency, as the shells could easily be strung together.

DENTALIUM ELEPHANTINUM

AUTHORITY: (Linnaeus 1758)
COMMON NAME: Elephant's tusk
GENERAL DESCRIPTION: The popularity of the elephant s tusk shell among collectors is due no doubt to its large size. Approximately 10 strong, rounded ribs run the whole length of the shell. It occurs throughout its range at depths from 6 to 150 feet (2–50m). It burrows down into the substrate of sand or mud, with the smaller end protruding above the surface. In common with all tusk shells, it is carnivorous, feeding on foraminifera and other micro-organisms.
DISTRIBUTION: South Philippines; Japan; North Australia

ANTALIS DENTALIS

AUTHORITY: (Linnaeus 1758)
COMMON NAME: European tusk shell
GENERAL DESCRIPTION: This shell is slightly curved and often traversed by strong longitudinal ridges. The shell normally white but may be pale brown or pink. The animal, which is white in colour normally occurs in colonies buried sandy substrates at depths below three fathoms. The shells are often washed ashore after storms.
DISTRIBUTION: Mediterranean; Adriatic

GLOSSARY

....

ductor scars – the impressions on the inner walls of bivalve
lls left by the muscles used by bivalves to close the shells.
erture – the opening at the front of a gastropod or razor shell.
ex – the point from which a shell begins to grow; the top of
spire of a gastropod shell.
ial – a term usually applied to gastropods to describe markings
whorls that follow, or are parallel to, the axis of the shell.
is – the imaginary line, drawn from the anterior to the apex of
tropods, around which a shell's whorls revolve.
ad – tiny, usually rounded knob, groups of which may be laid
ally, resembling a string of beads.
valve – a mollusc such as an oyster that has a hinged double
dy whorl – the largest and last formed section of a gastropod
ll; it encloses the soft parts of the creature.
ssus – tuft of silky filaments by which some molluscs adhere
rocks.
lcareous – made of, or containing, calcium carbonate (chalk)
l usually having a white appearance.
ncellate – marked with crossing lines that form a lattice-like
tern.
ncellation – an area sculptured by lines – ridges and threads,
example – crossing each other at right angles; also referred to
eticulation.
rdinal – a projection below the umbo on the hinge plate of a
alve.
rina – a structure or part of a structure that resembles a keel
ridge.
itin – the substance that forms the horny constituent in the
skeleton of arthropods.
iton – a mollusc with a shell formed of eight overlapping
.es.
lumella – the spirally twisting pillar surrounding the axis of a
tropod shell, which is visible in the aperture.
rd – a rope-like, usually spiral ornamentation on a gastropod
ll.
rneous – hornlike or horny; made of chitin.
ronated – crown-like; bearing nodules on the shoulder or
e.
ntate or Denticulate – toothed or bearing tooth-like notches.
nticle – a small, tooth-like, usually rounded projection; shells
h denticles around the margins or inside the lip are described
dentate" or "denticulate".
rsum – the back of a shell, opposite to the aperture.
siform – shaped like a spindle; rounded and broadest in the
dle and tapering towards each end.
bose – rounded or spherical; like a ball.
el – a raised, often sharp edge or carina.

Lamella – thin plate or scale.
Lamellate – covered in lamellae or scales.
Lip – the inside or outside edge of the aperture of a gastropod
shell.
Maculate – marked with irregular spots or blotches.
Mantle – the glandular flap or fold of the body wall of a mollusc
that secretes the shell-forming material.
Nacreous – of or like mother-of-pearl.
Nodular or Nodulose or Nodulous – bearing or decorated
with nodules.
Nodule – a sharp or rounded knob; a lumpy protuberance.
Operculum – the oval or round structure, which may be cal-
careous or corneous, on the foot of many species of gastropods,
which is used to close the aperture when the creature withdraws
into its shell.
Ovate – egg-shaped or oval.
Pallial sinus – a curved scar line visible on the interior walls of
bivalve shells at the point where the edges of the mantle were
attached.
Parietal – the area or wall, sometimes referred to as the inner
lip, in a gastropod shell that lies opposite the outer lip and above
the columella.
Periostracum – the fibrous, skin-like membrane that covers
many live shells.
Plicate – having parallel folds, like a fan; usually used to describe
the plaited or folded portion of the columella.
Plication – a fold.
Porcellaneous – having a porcelain- or china-like appearance.
Protoconch – the tip or apex of a gastropod shell, formed
during the creature's larval stage.
Radial – the ray-like ornamentation or sculpturing diverting
from the umbo of a bivalve shell.
Radula – a ribbon-like structure with rows of teeth, used by
molluscs to tear up food and take it to the mouth.
Reticulate – a net-like pattern of intersecting ridges or striations.
Siphonal canal – the tube-like structure used to protect the
fleshy tube of gastropods and bivalves that is used for drawing in
or ejecting liquid; it is situated at the front (base) of the aperture.
Spinose or Spinous – bearing or covered in spines. **Trochoidal**
– shaped like a spinning top.
Tubercle – a small rounded projection.
Umbilicus – the open point at the base of a gastropod shell
around which the body whorl is coiled.
Umbo (plural **Umbones**) – the part of a bivalve shell that was
formed first; it is also known as a beak.
Varix (plural **Varices**) – a rib-like thickening, representing a
growth resting stage, which appears as a raised ridge.
Whorl – one complete coil about the axis of a gastropod shell.